Be Calm

Barbara Freethy

Also available in the *Be Coloring* series:

Be Free

Be Happy

Be Creative

Be Industrious

In Stillness, the World is Restored.

~ Buddhist Proverb

Illustrated Contents

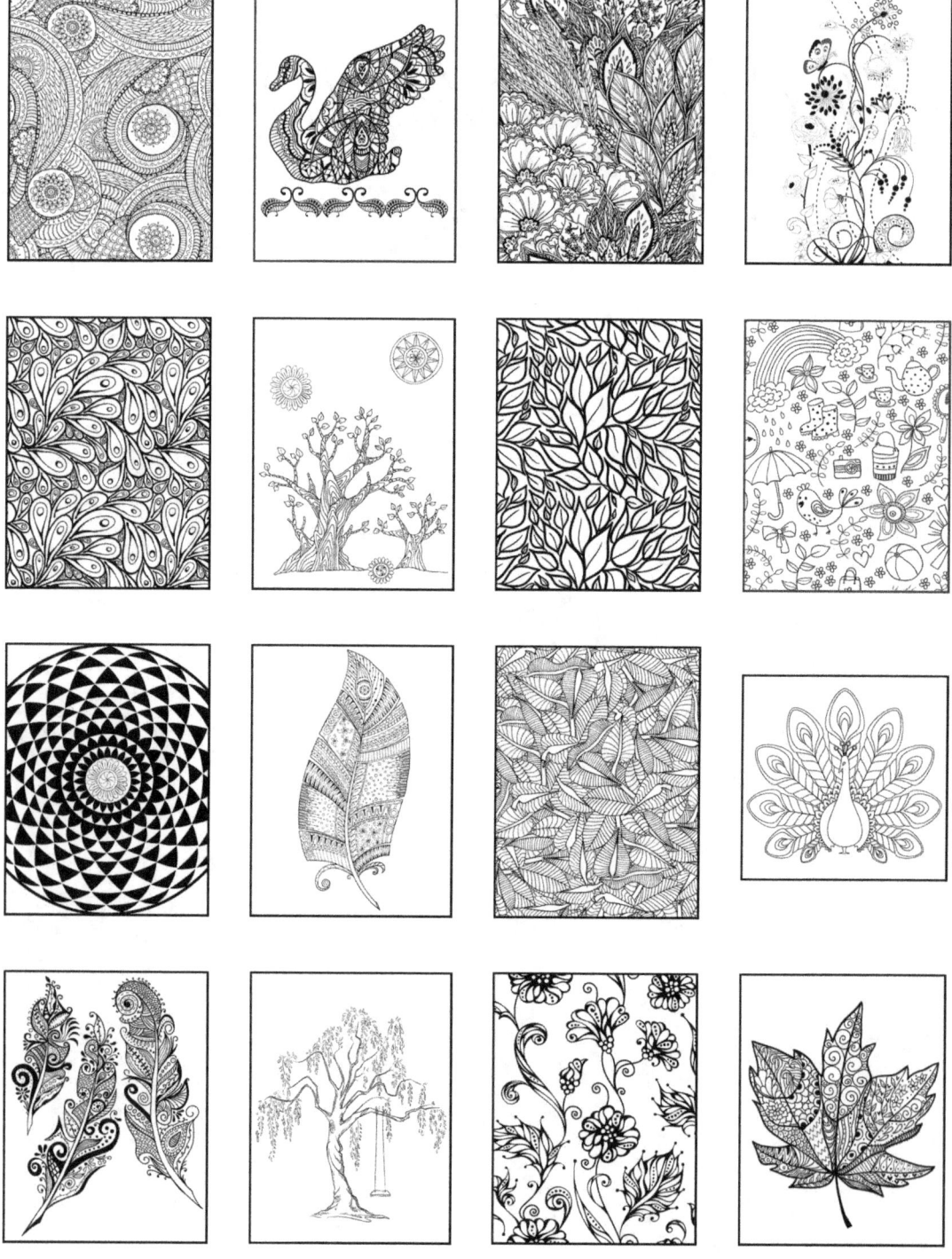

Illustrated Contents

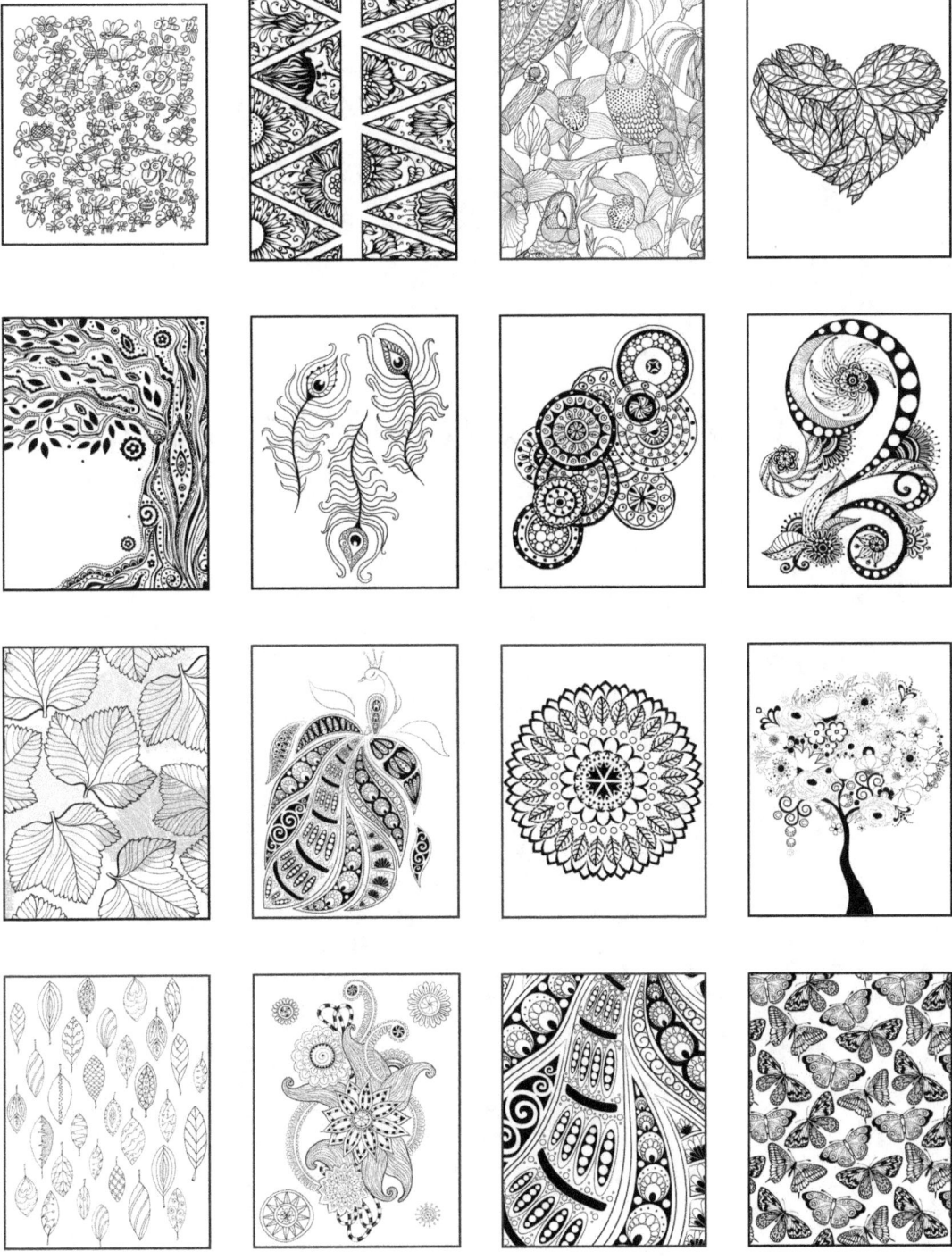

The obstacle is the path.

~ Zen Proverb

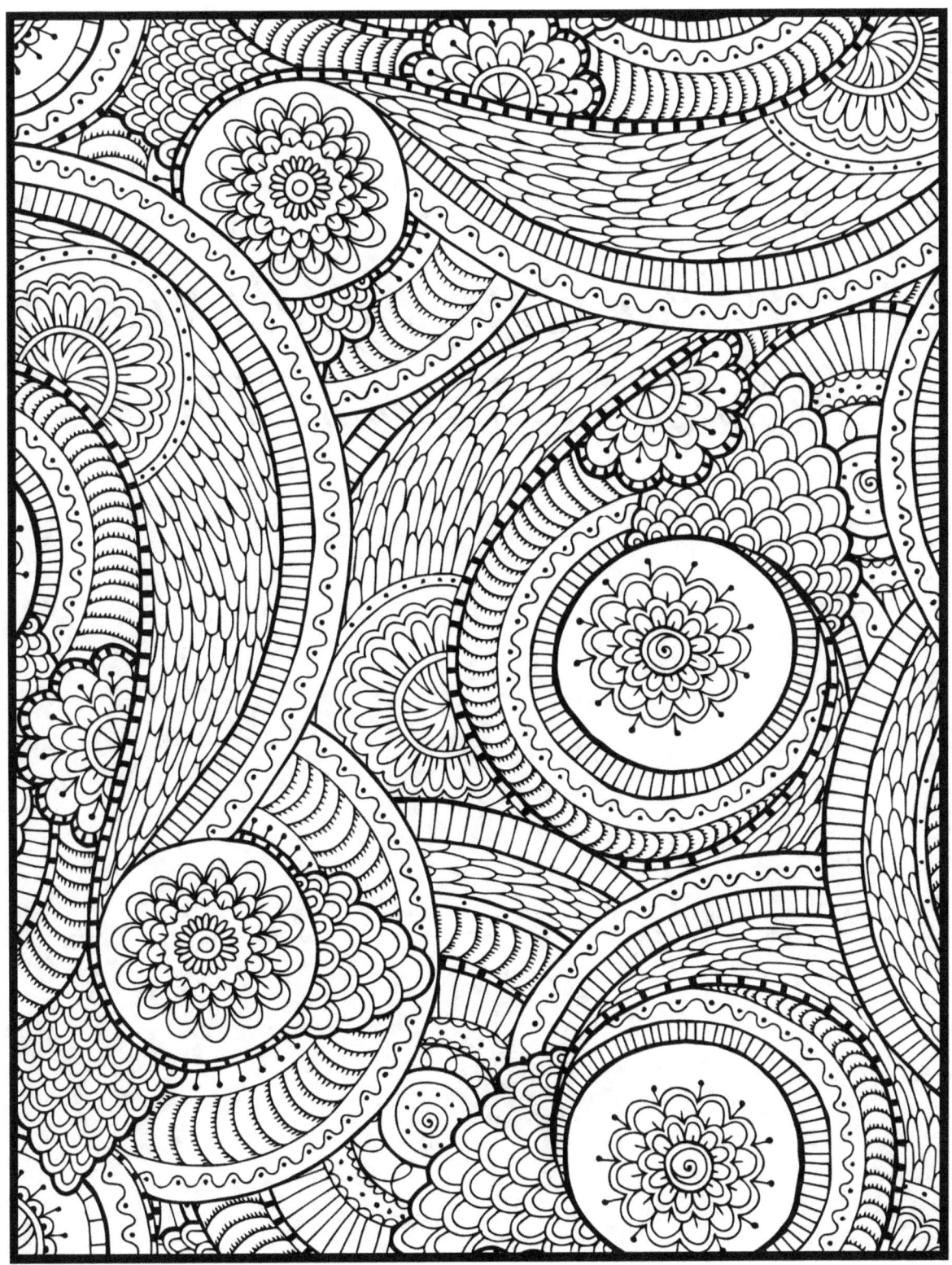

When Sleeping Woman Wakes, Mountain Moves.

~ African Proverb

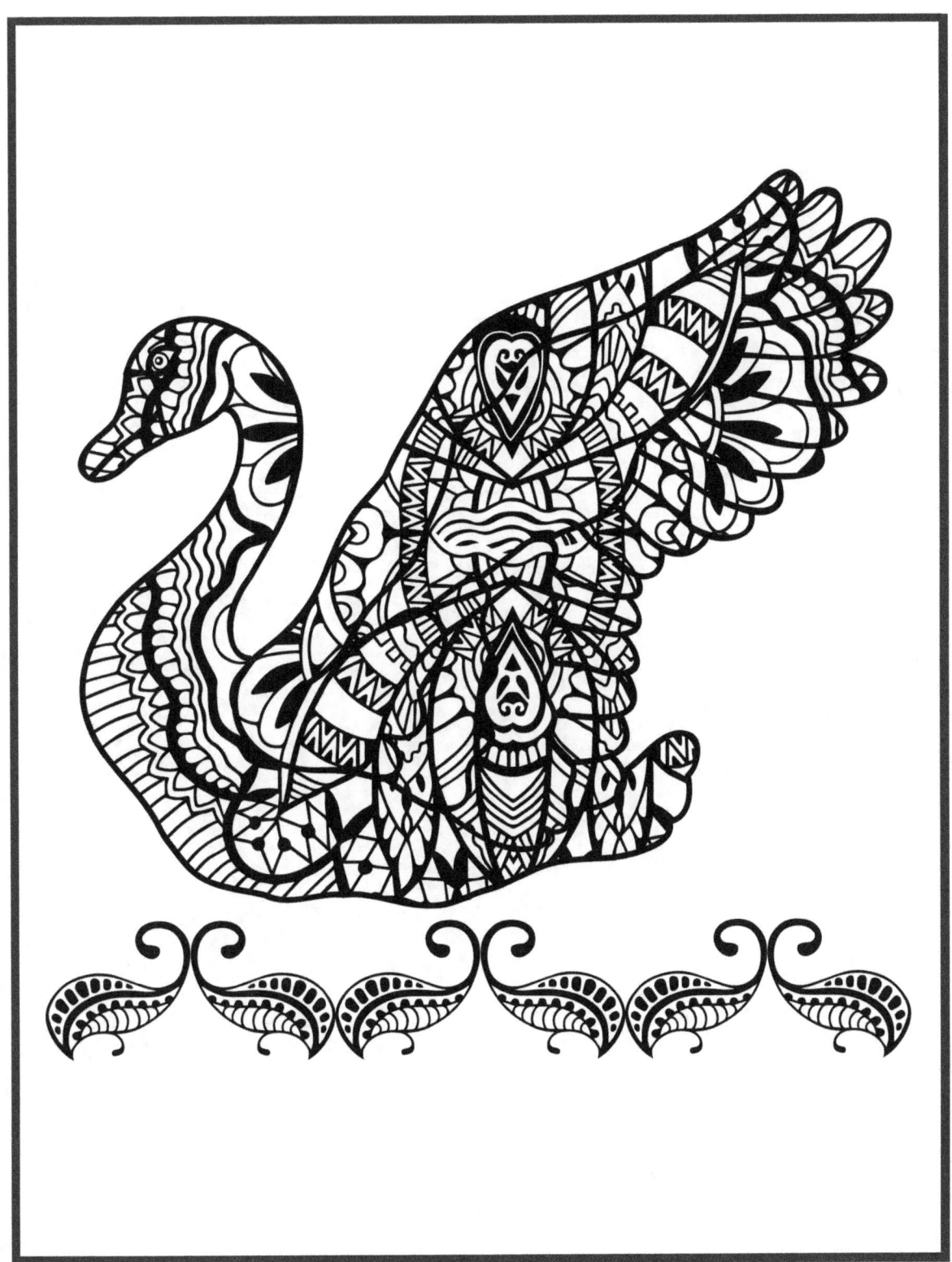

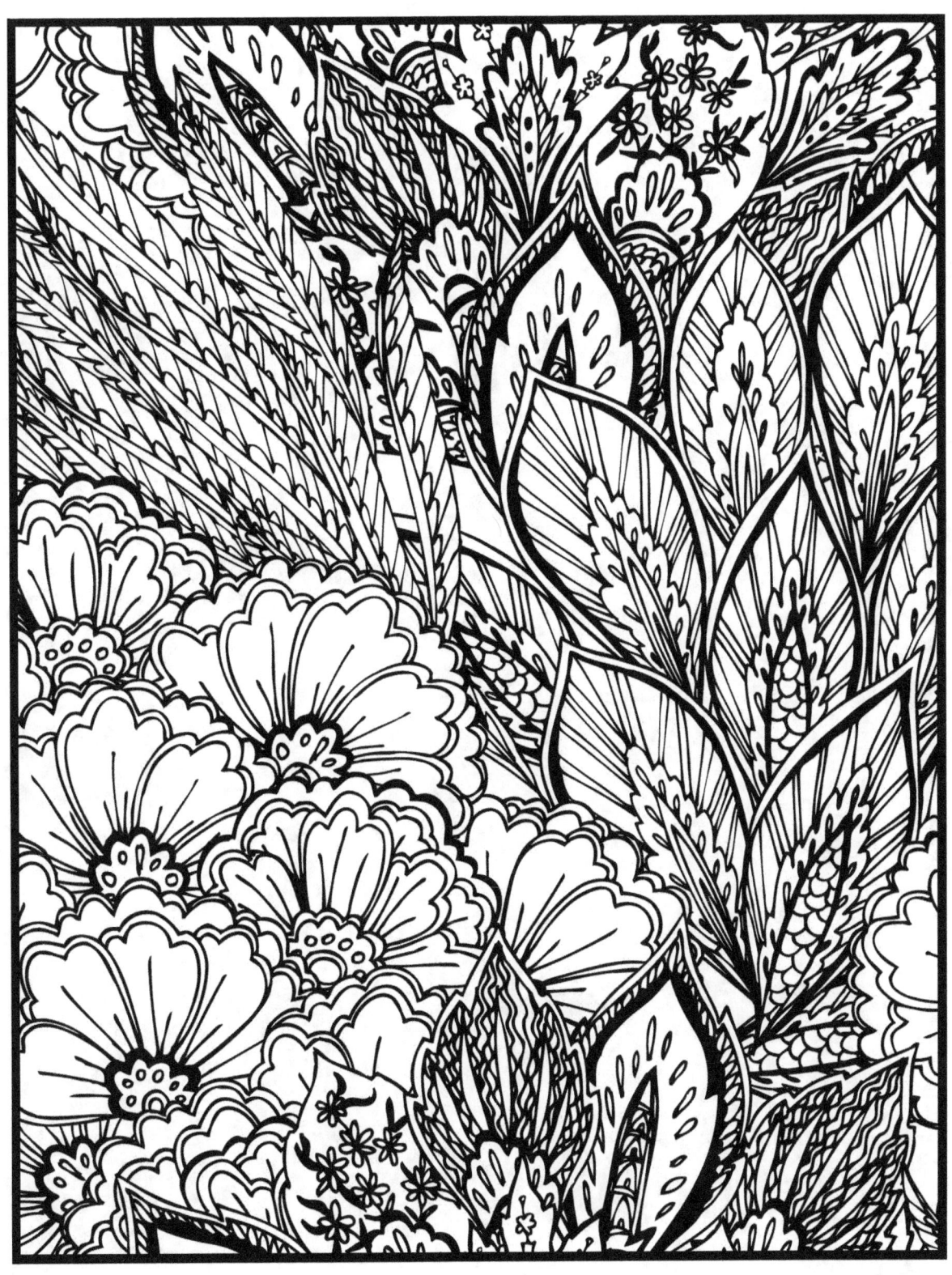

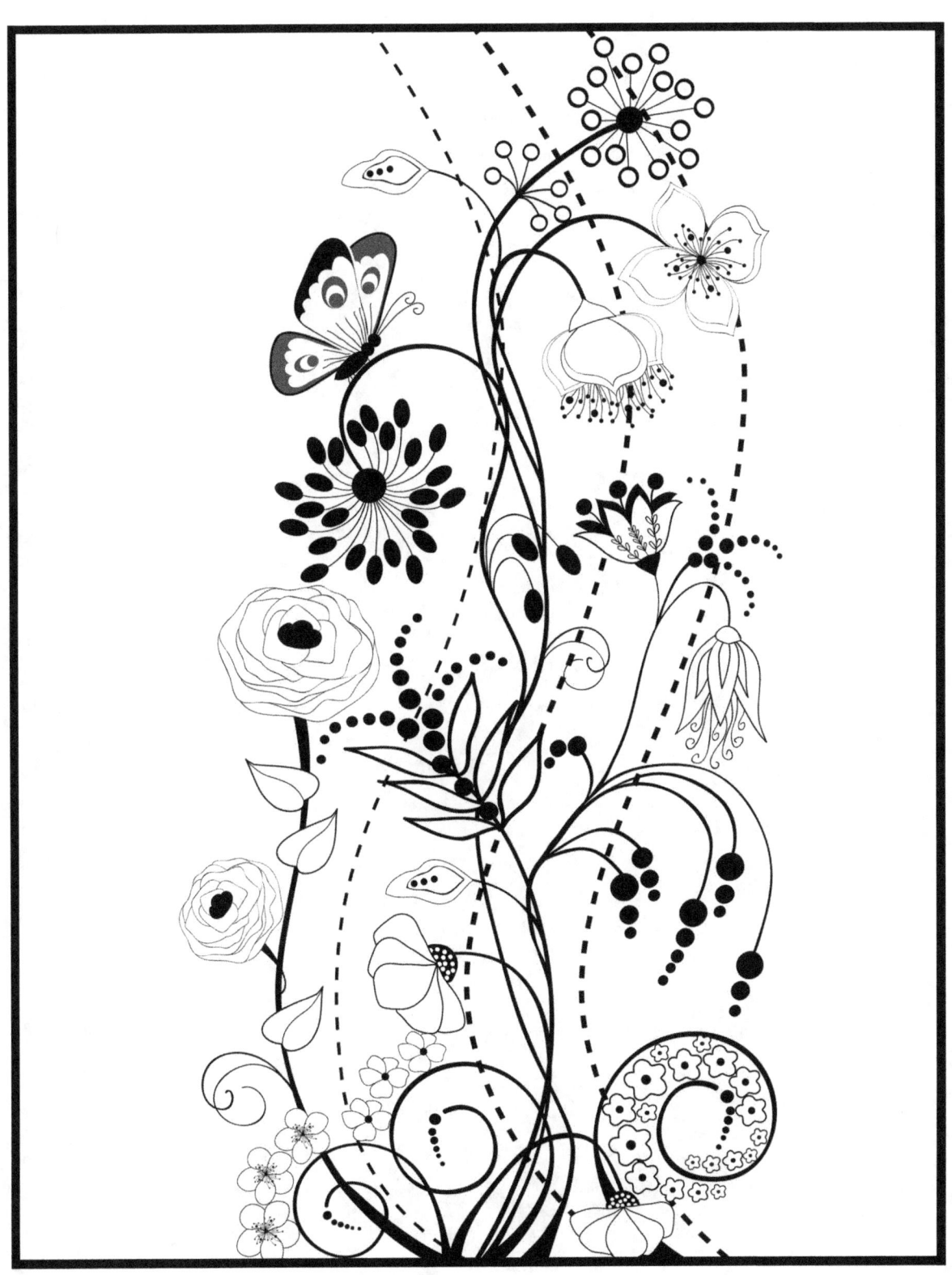

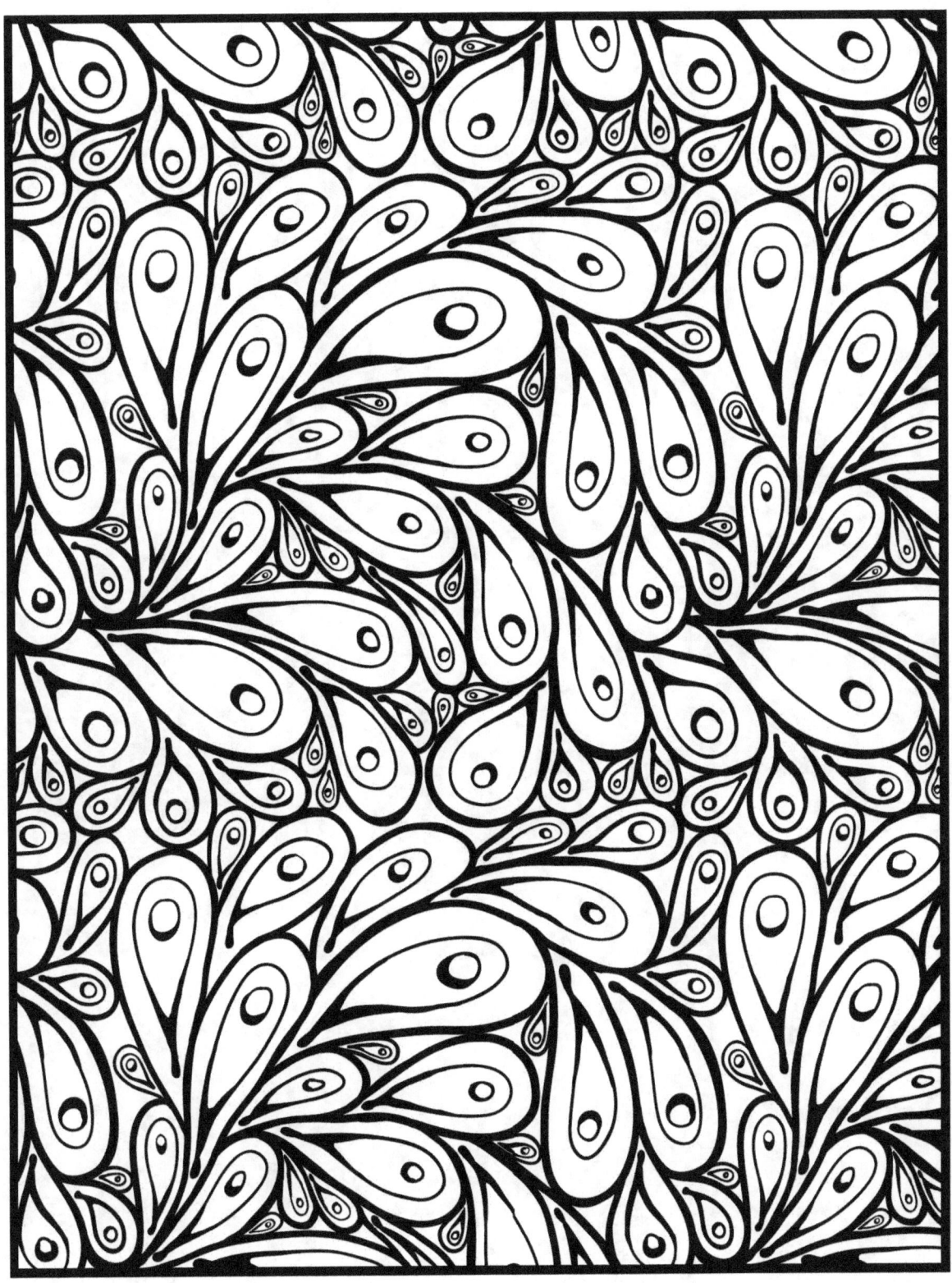

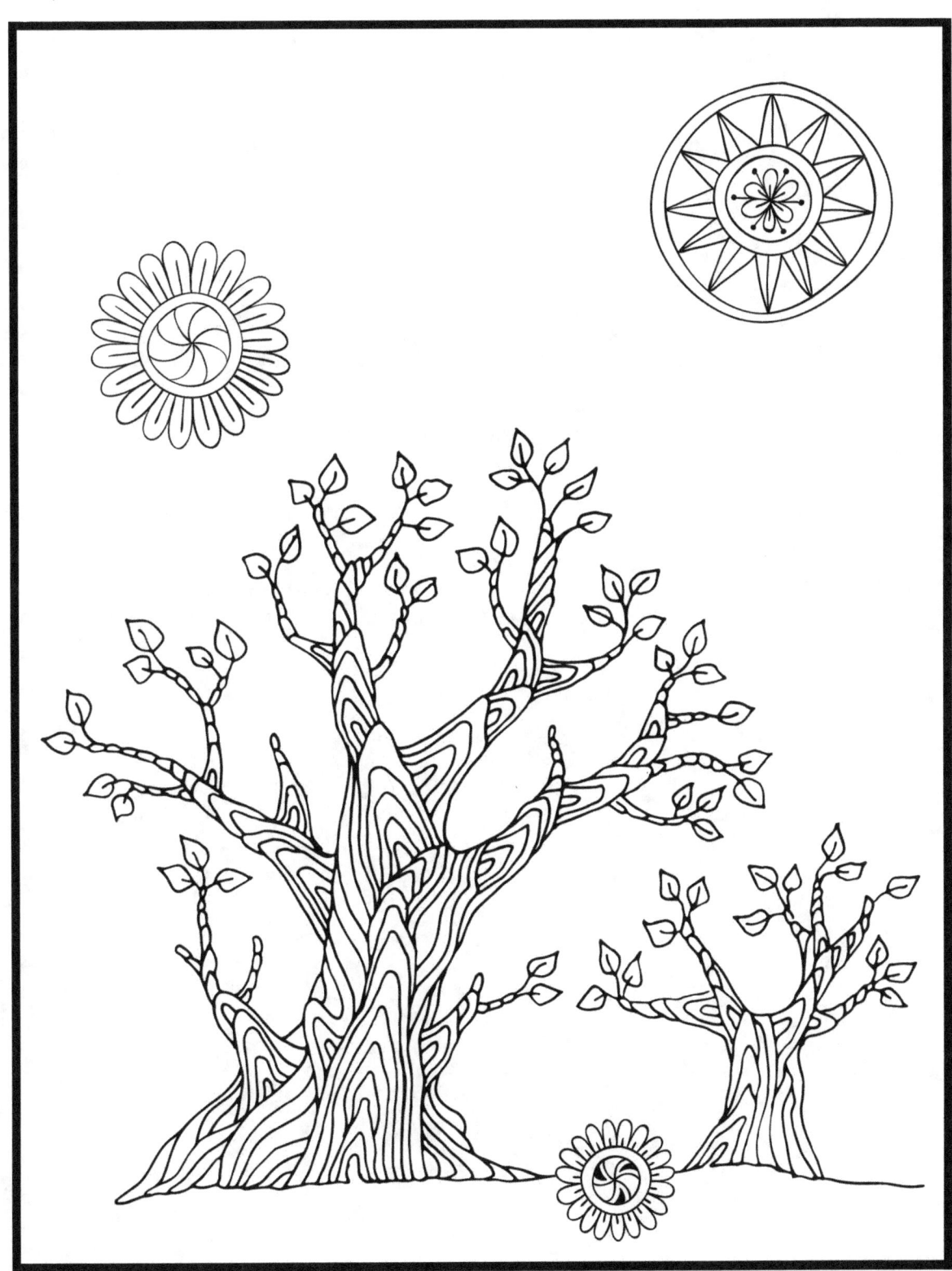

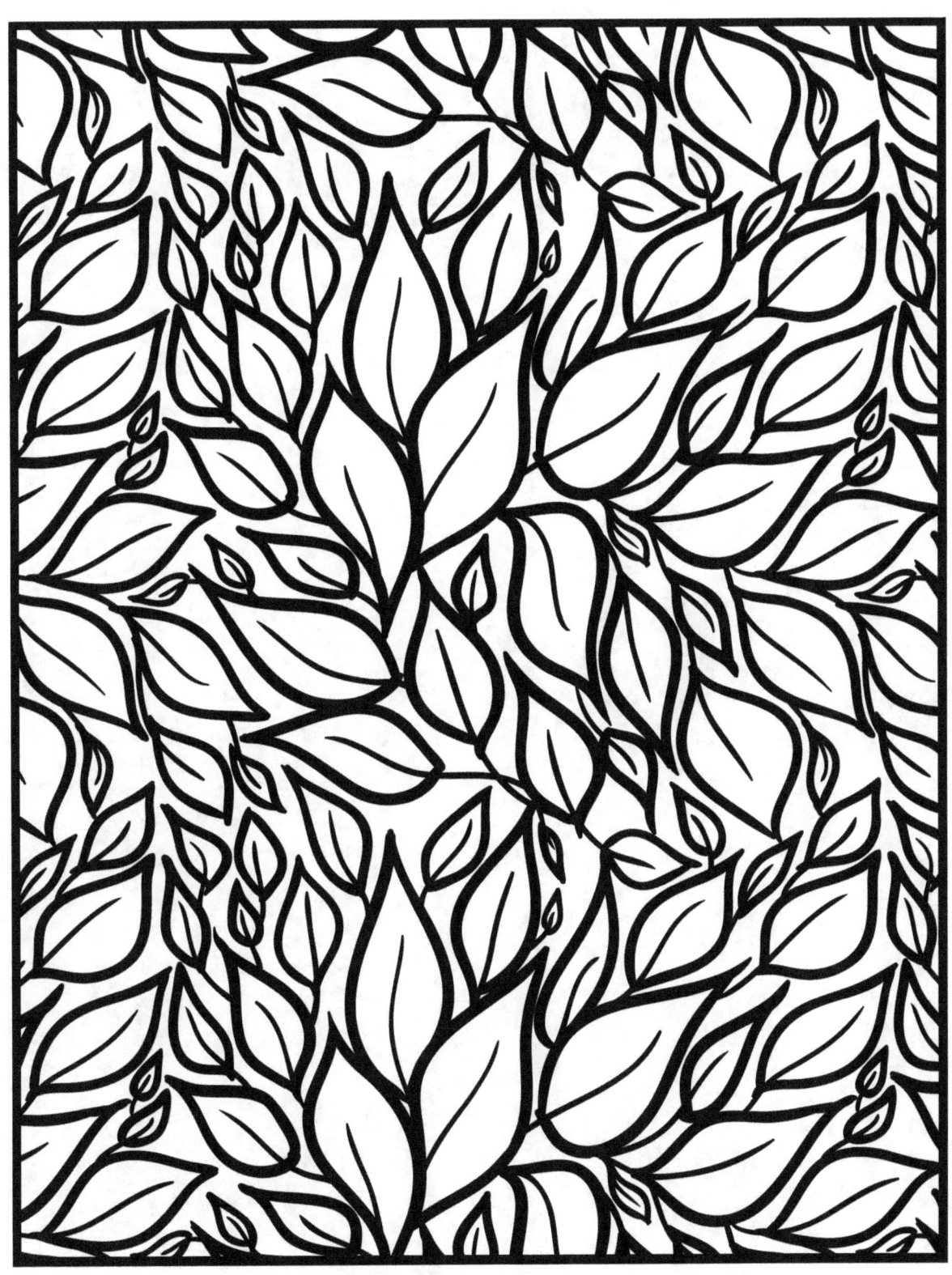

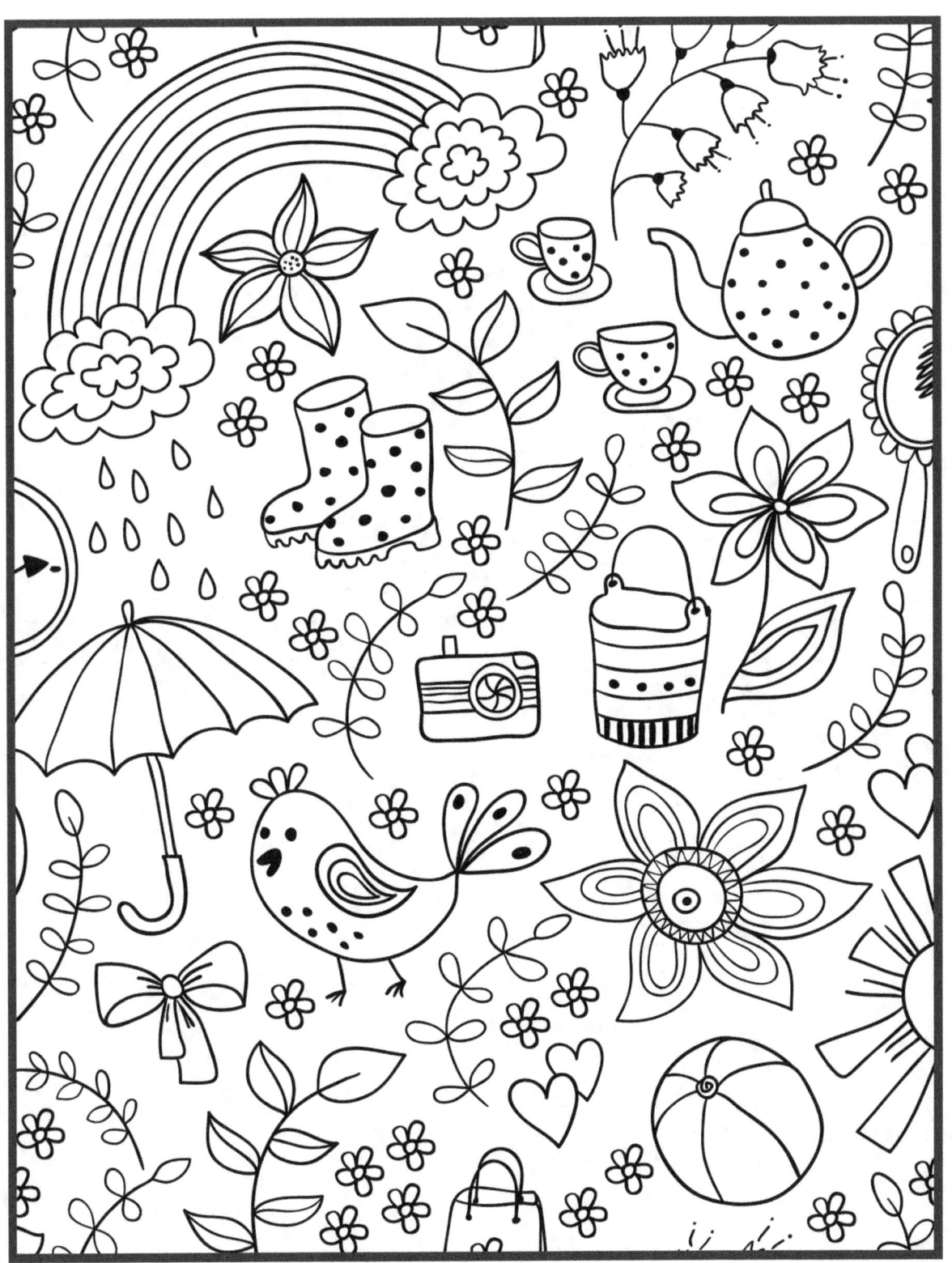

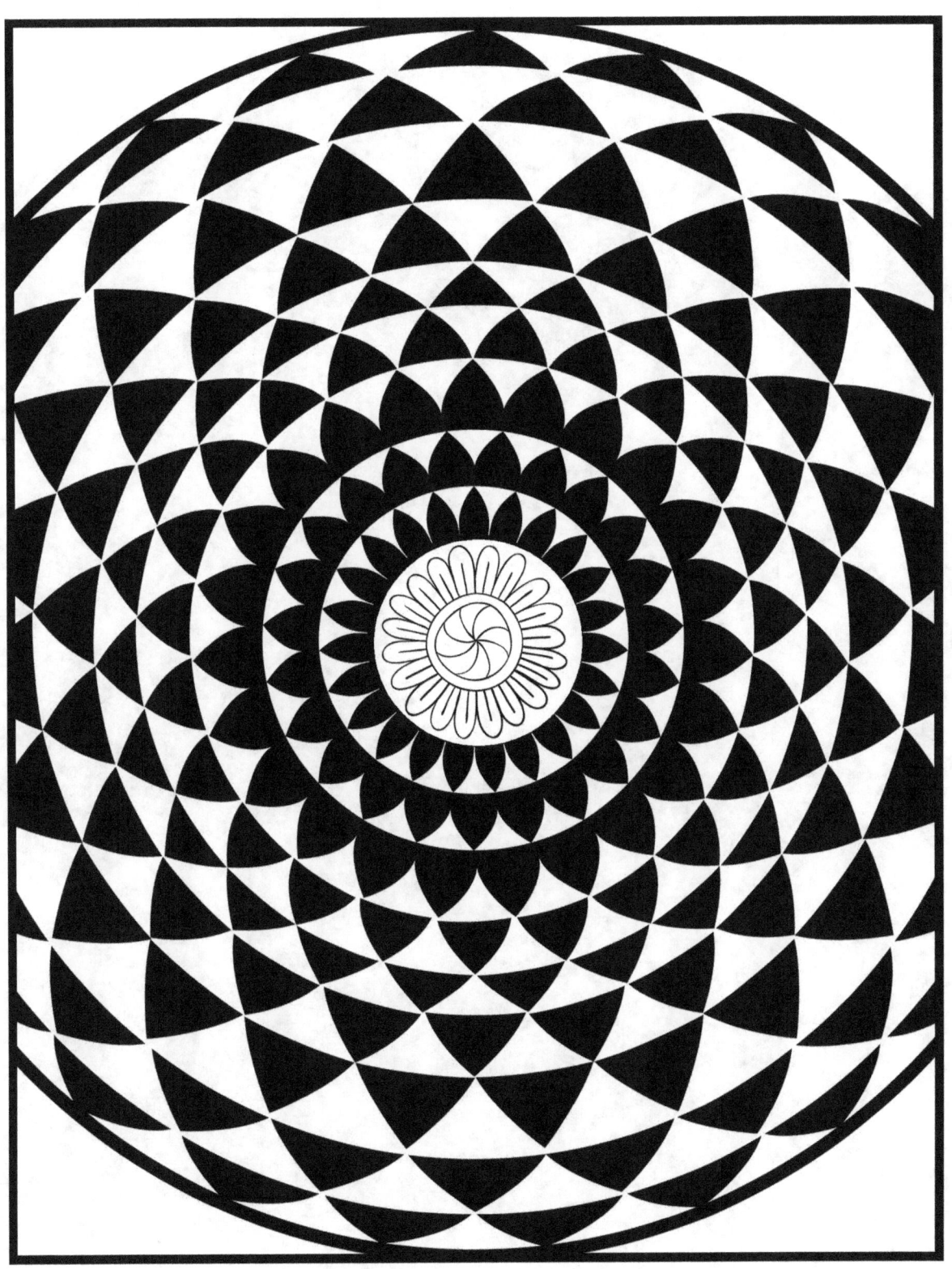

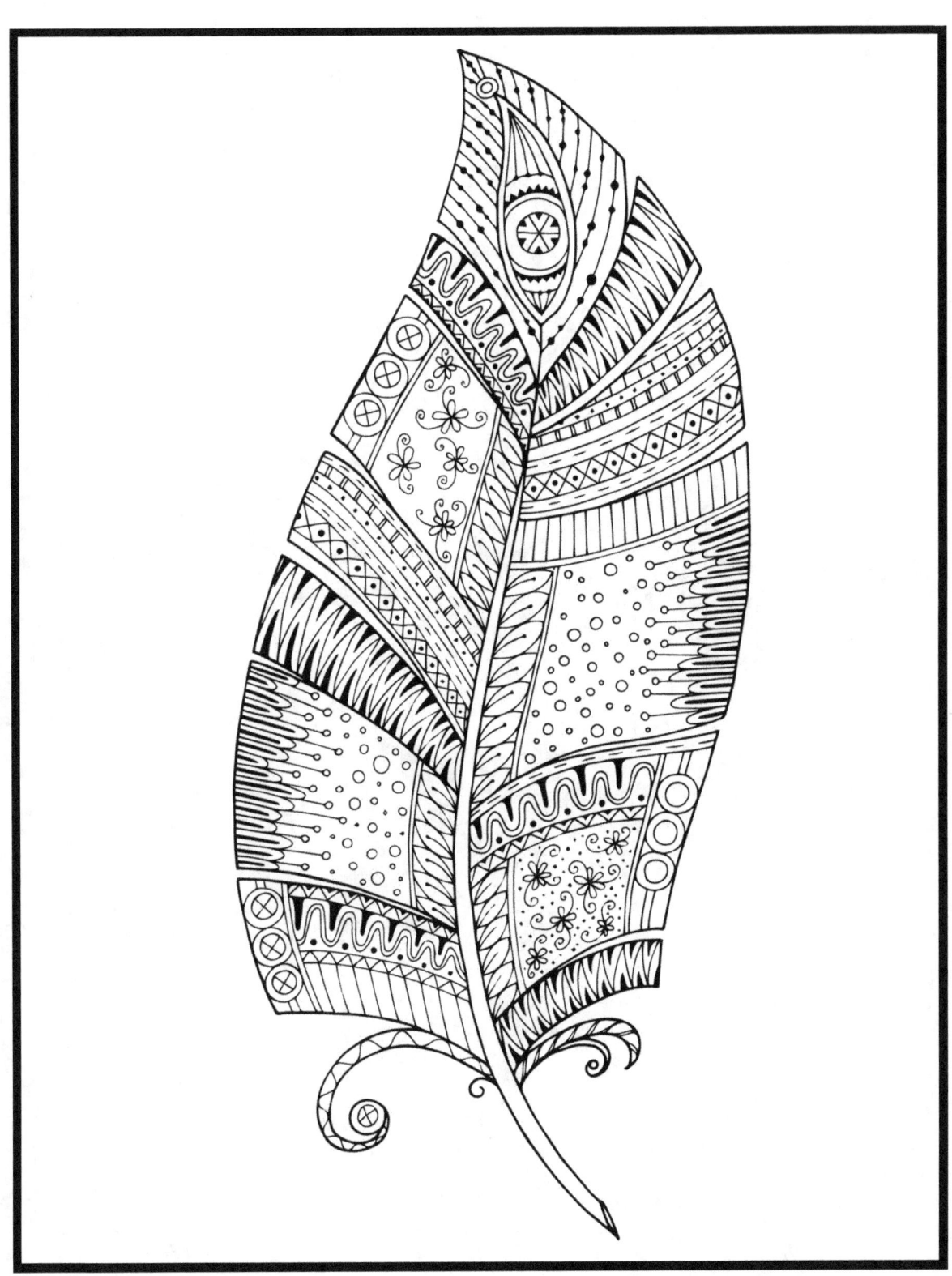

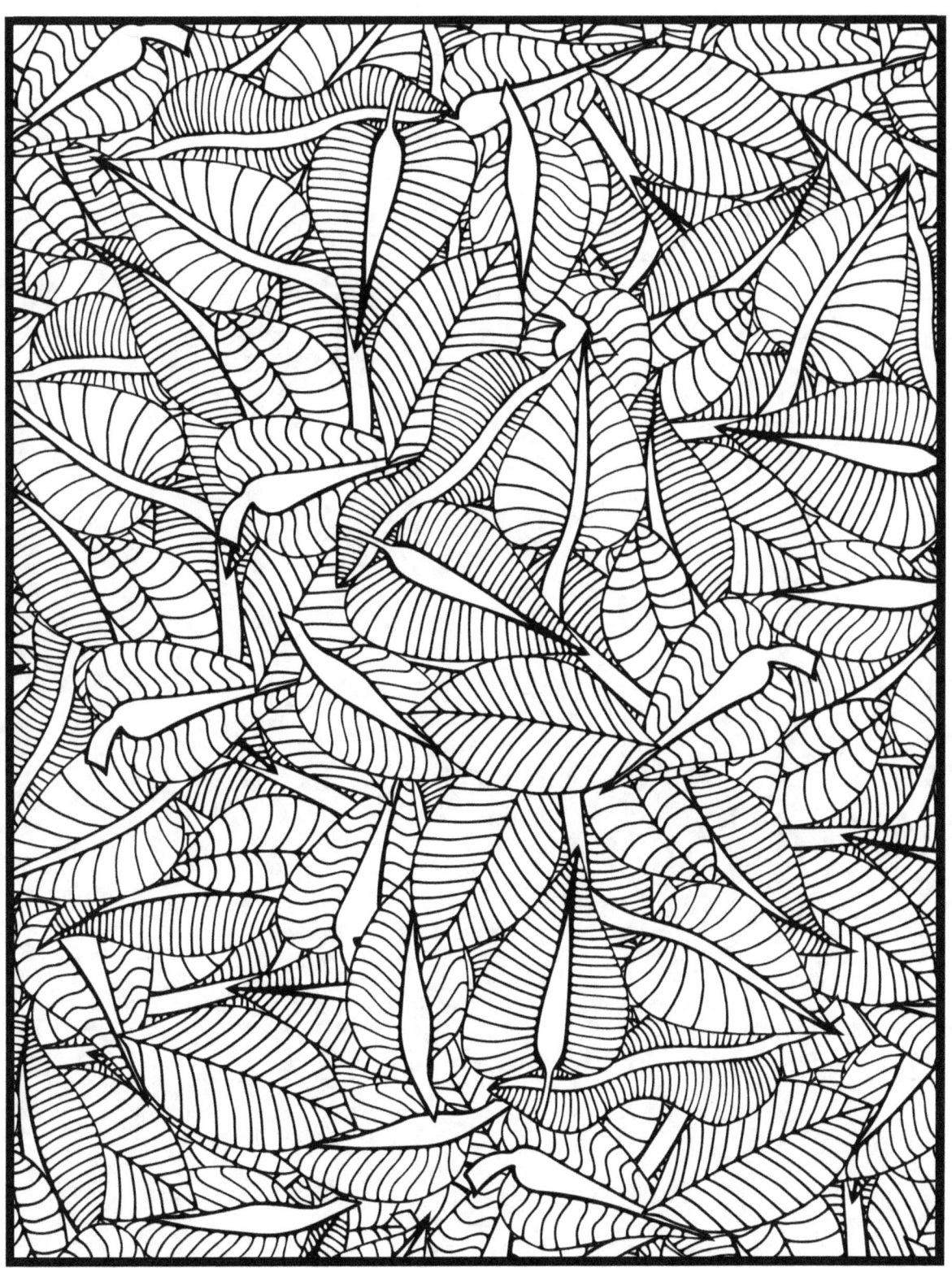

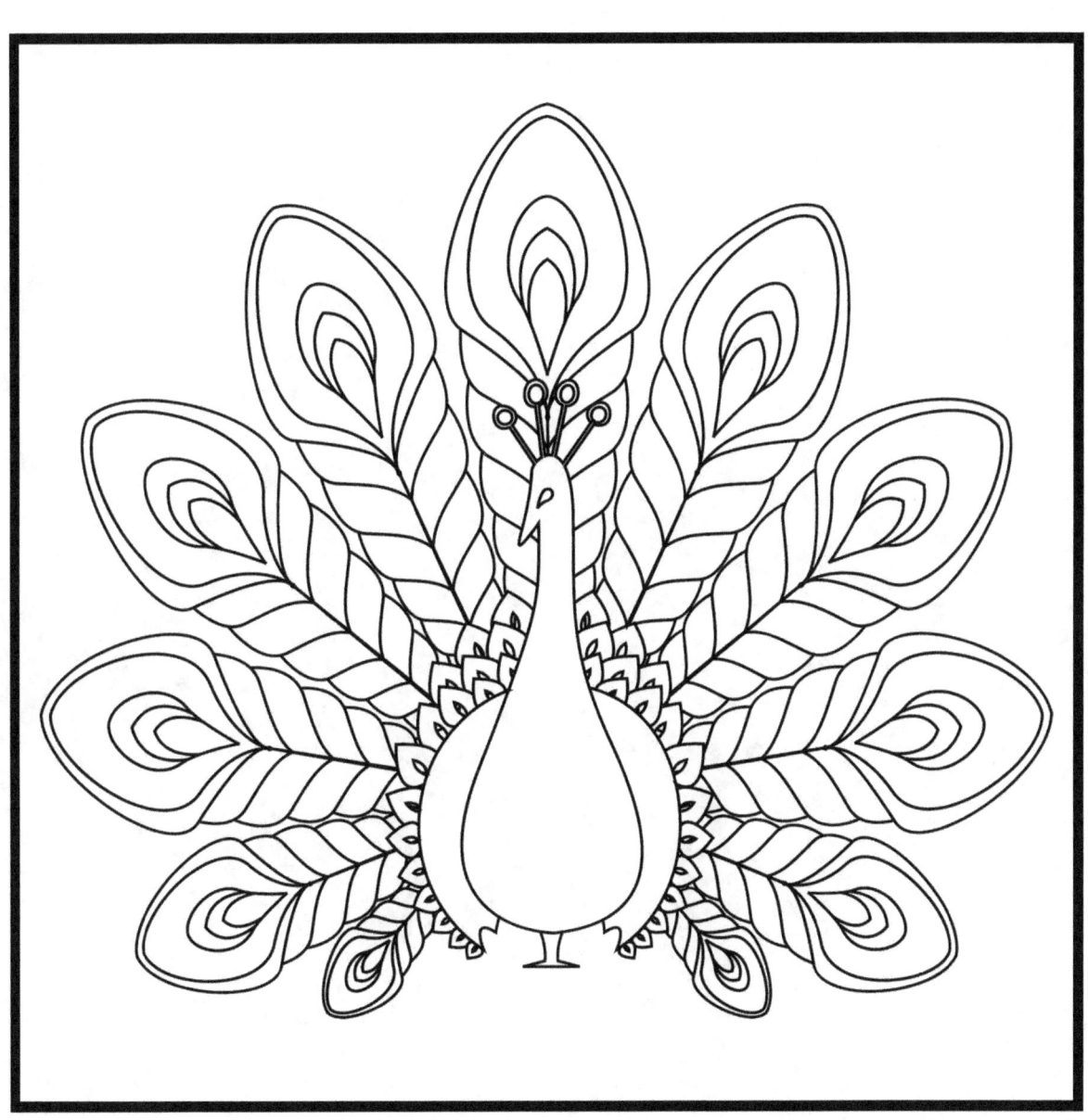

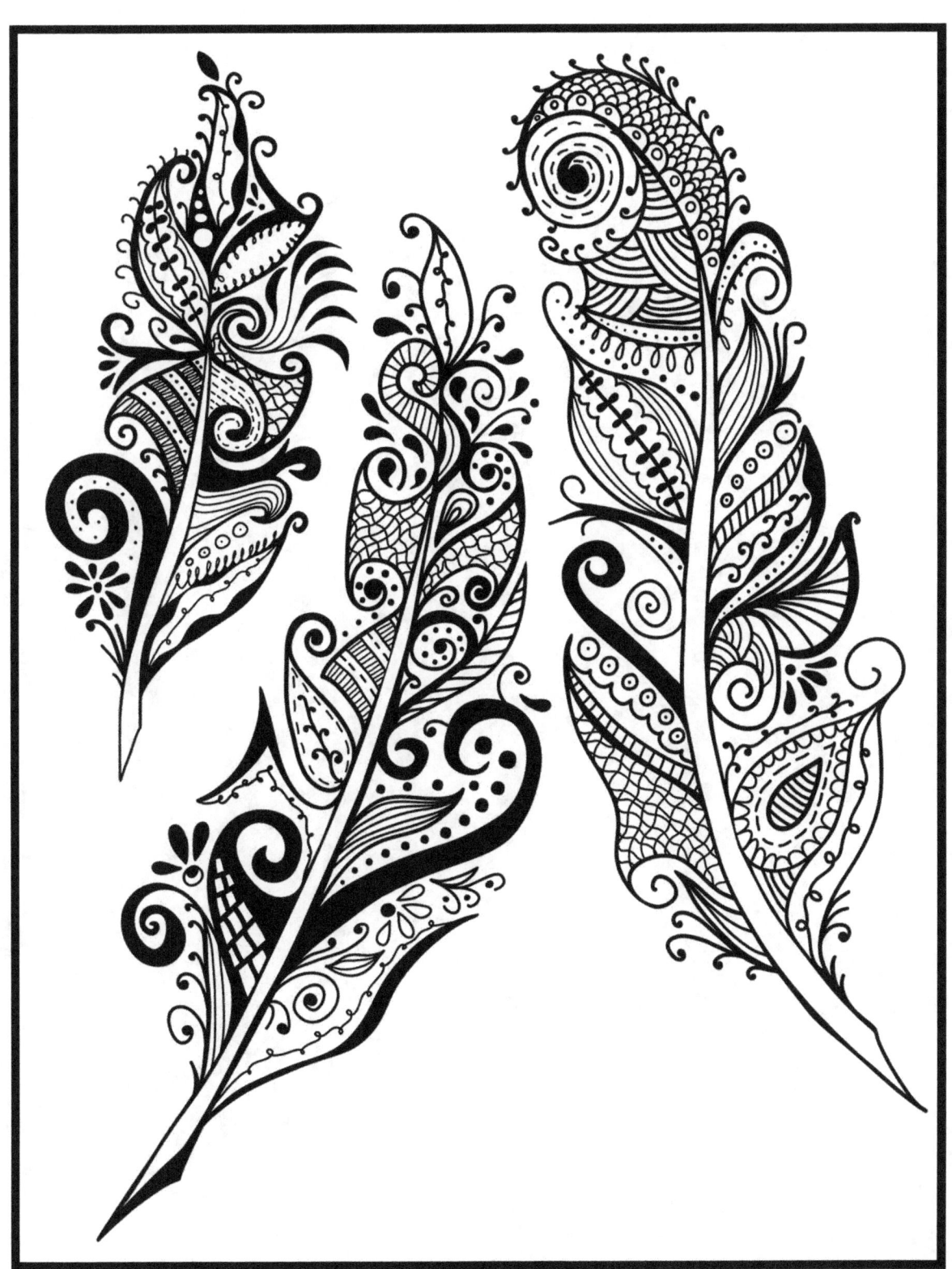

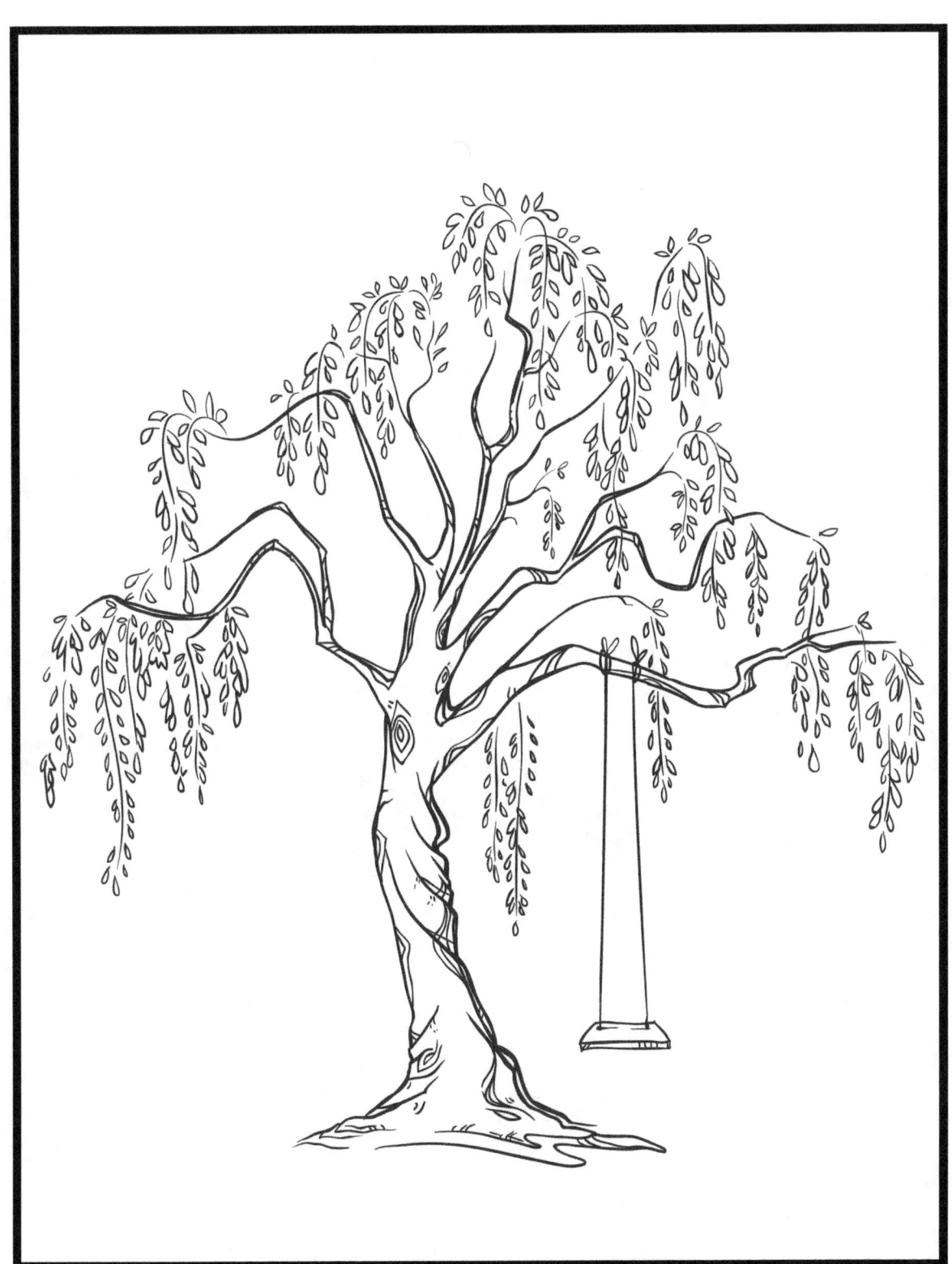

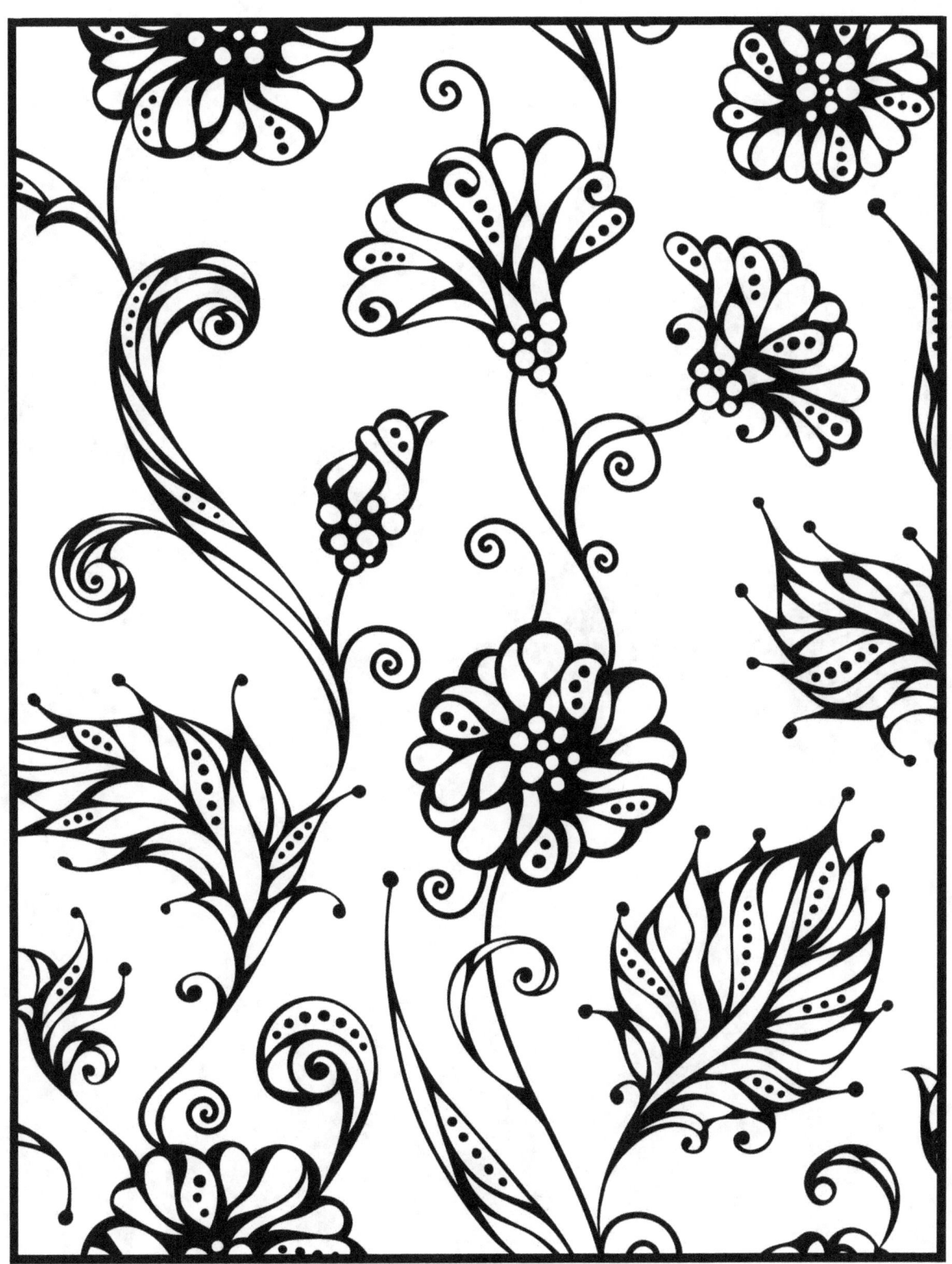

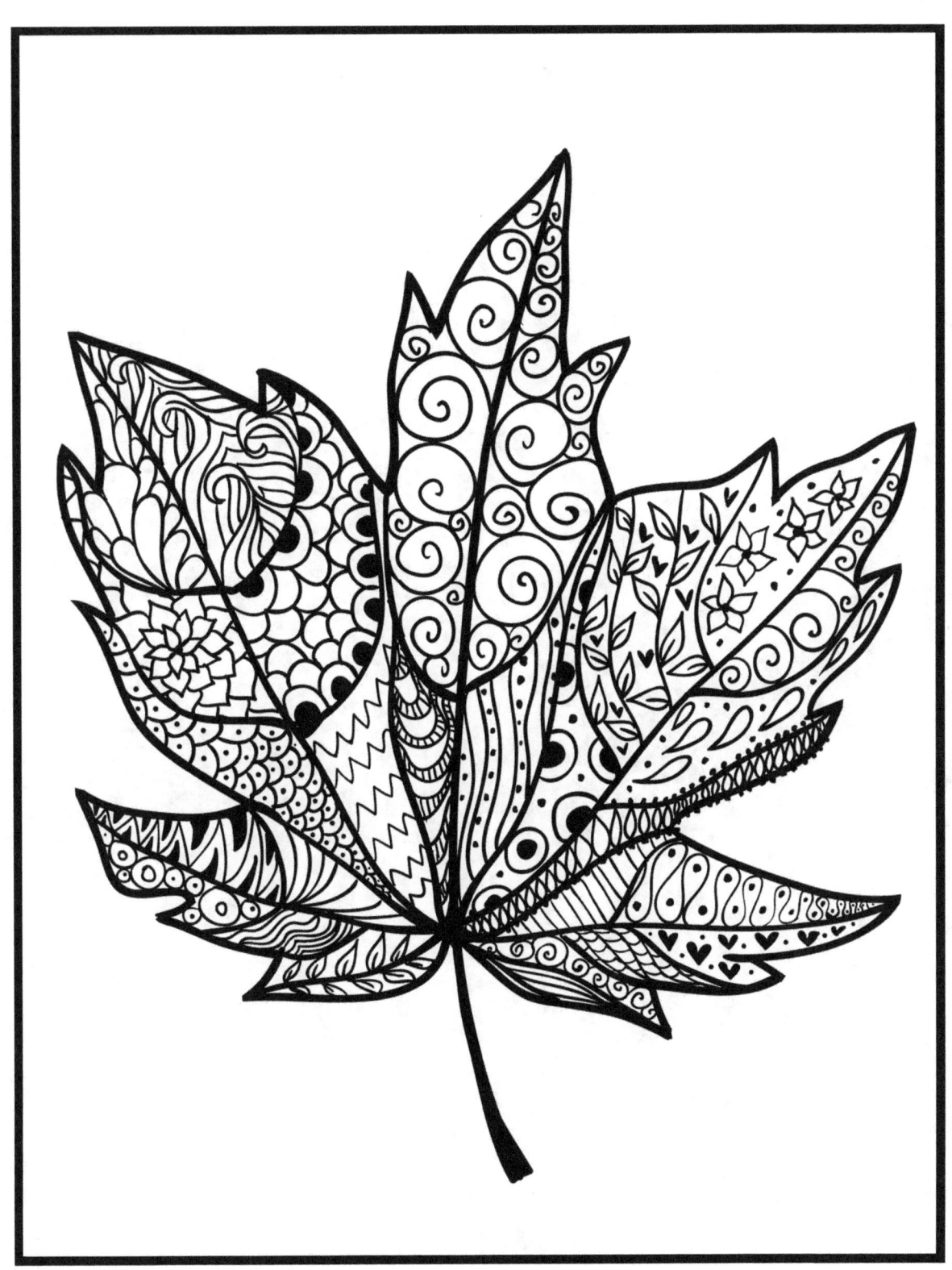

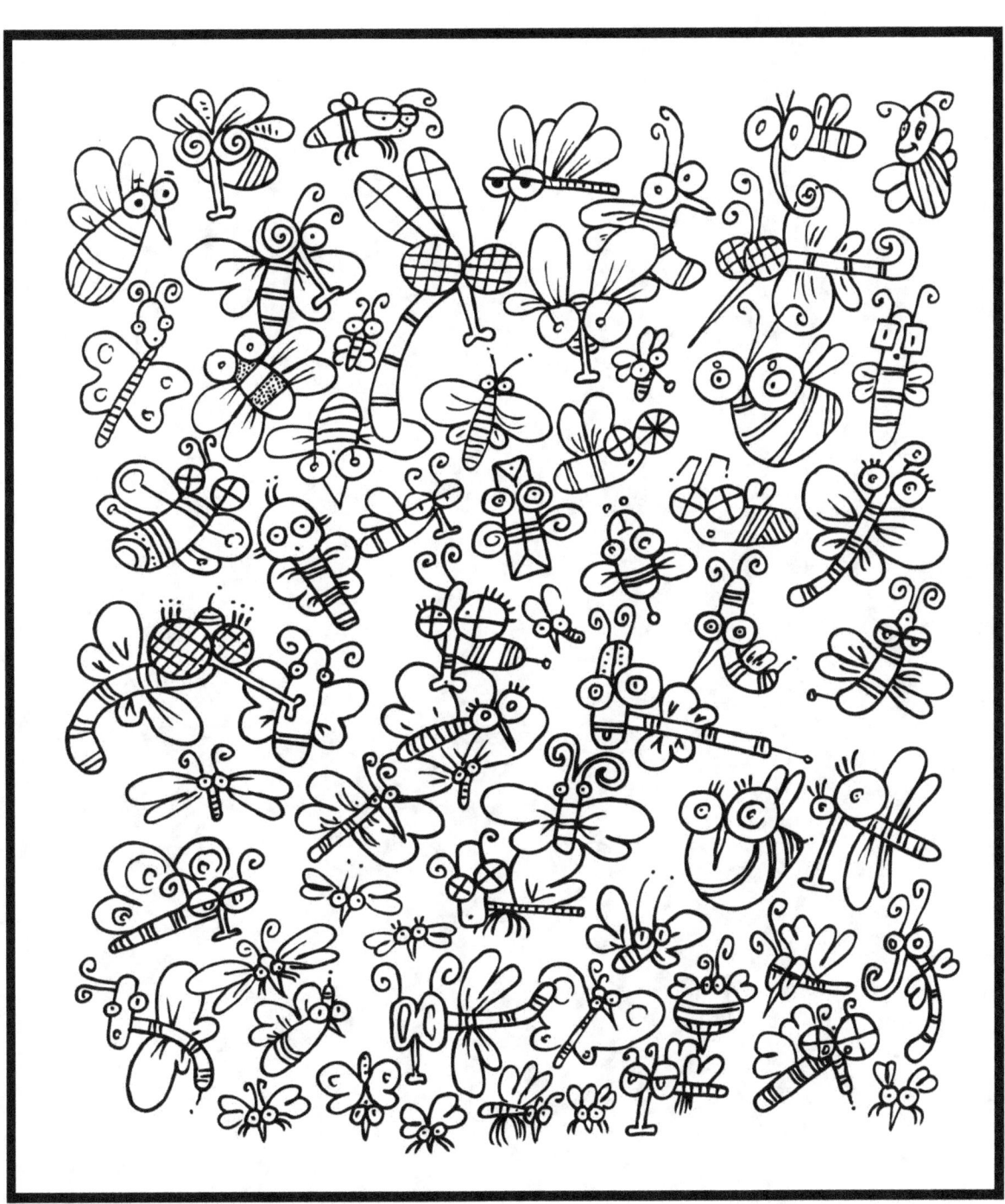

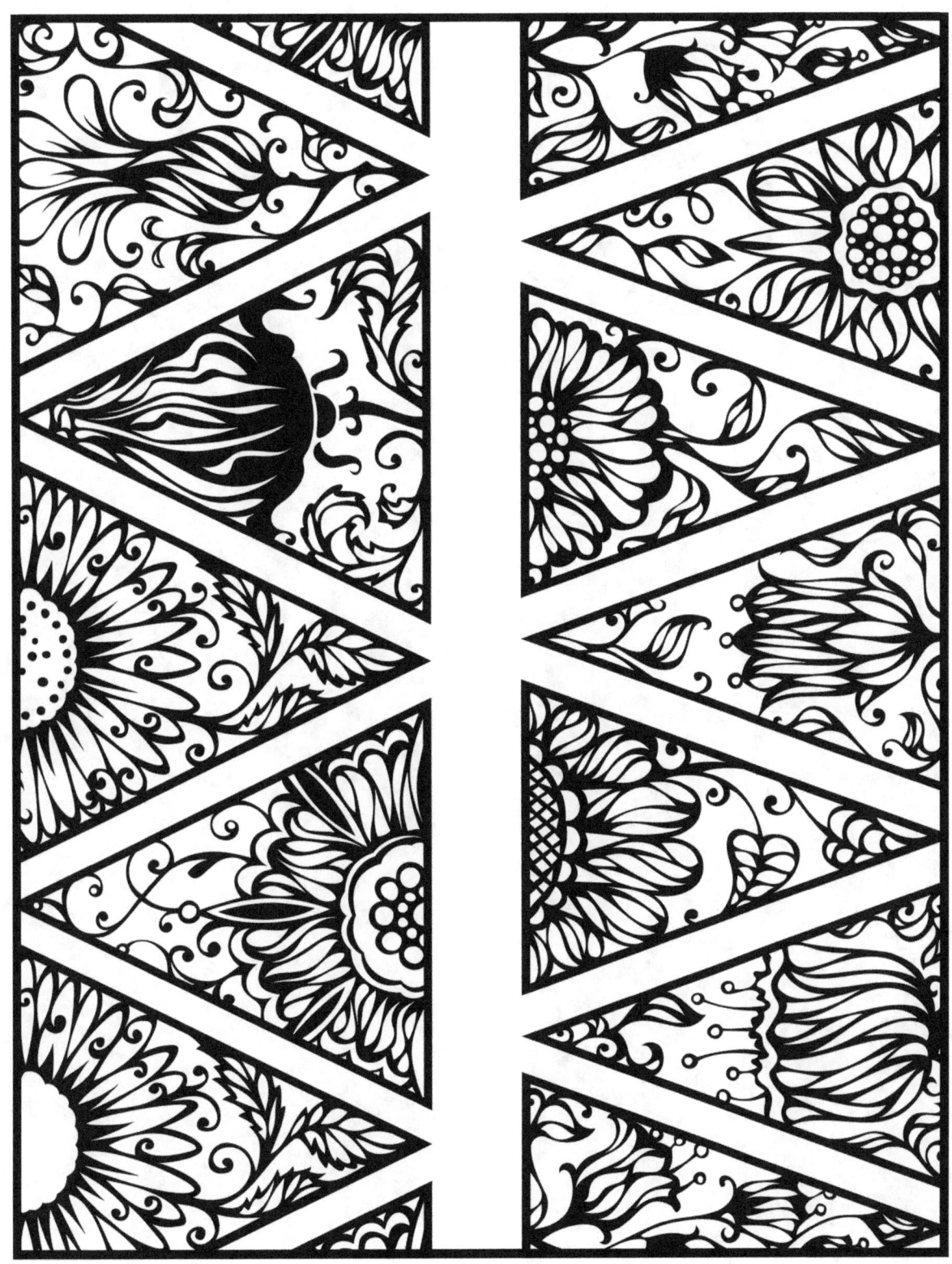

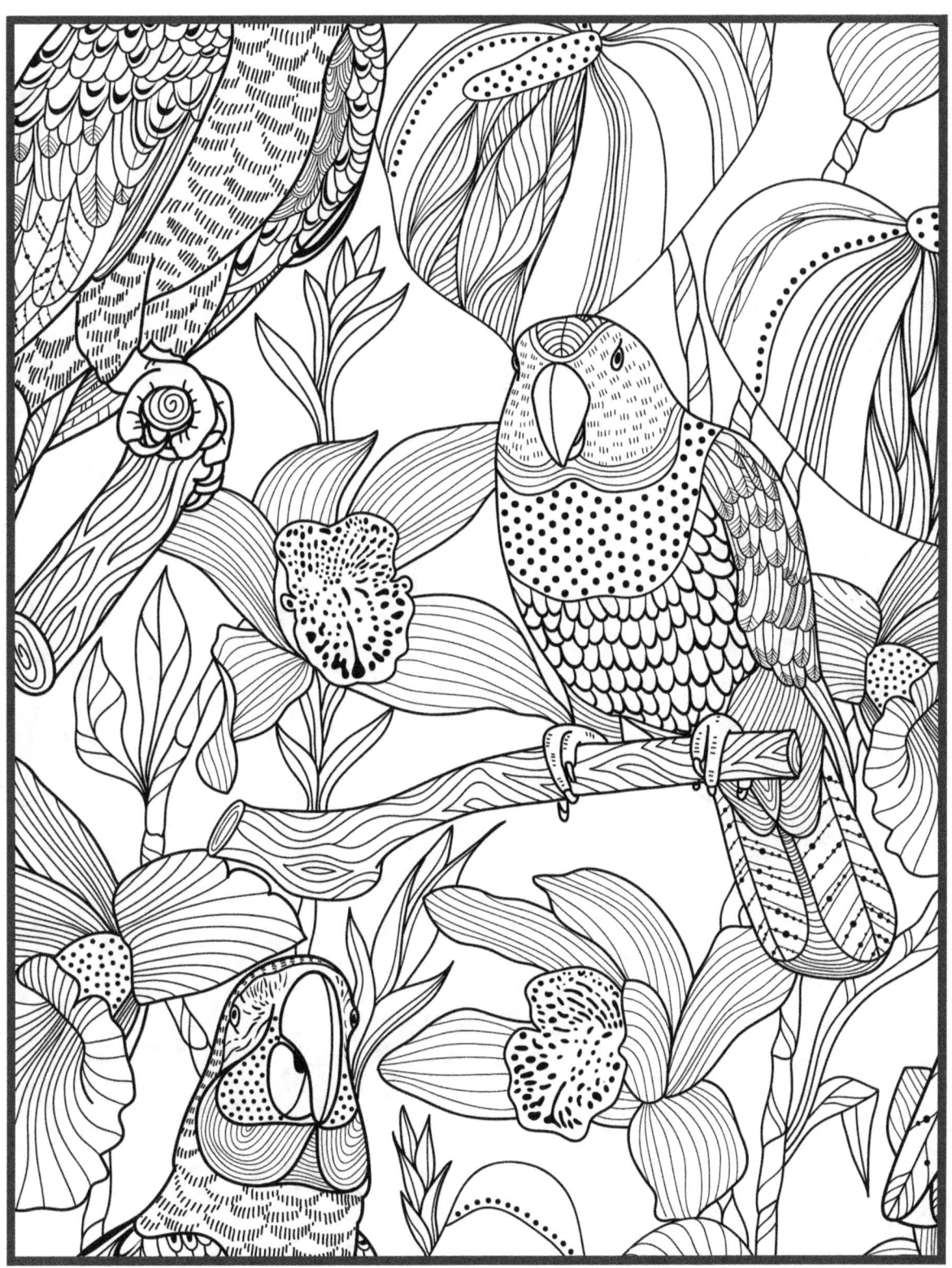

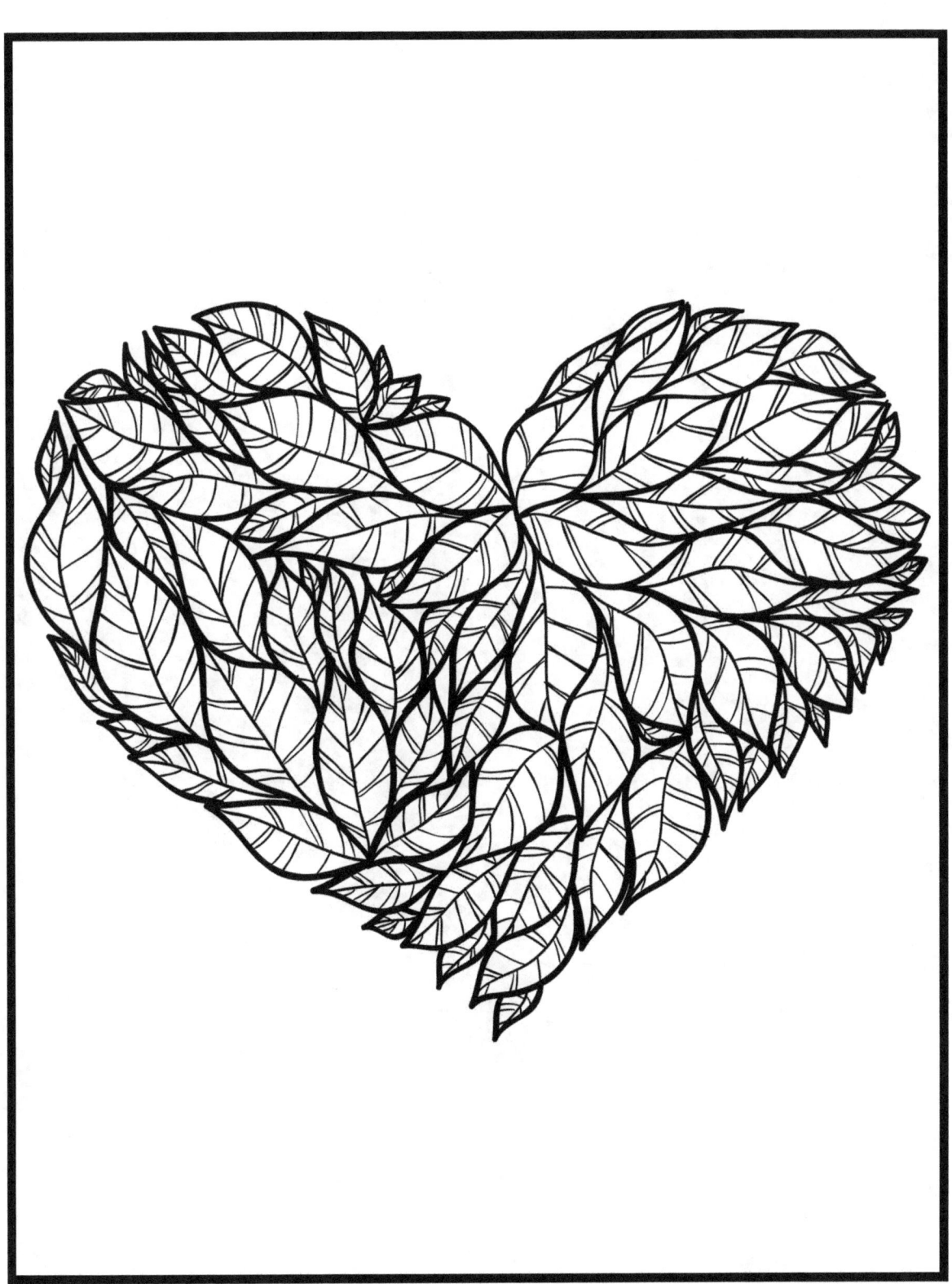

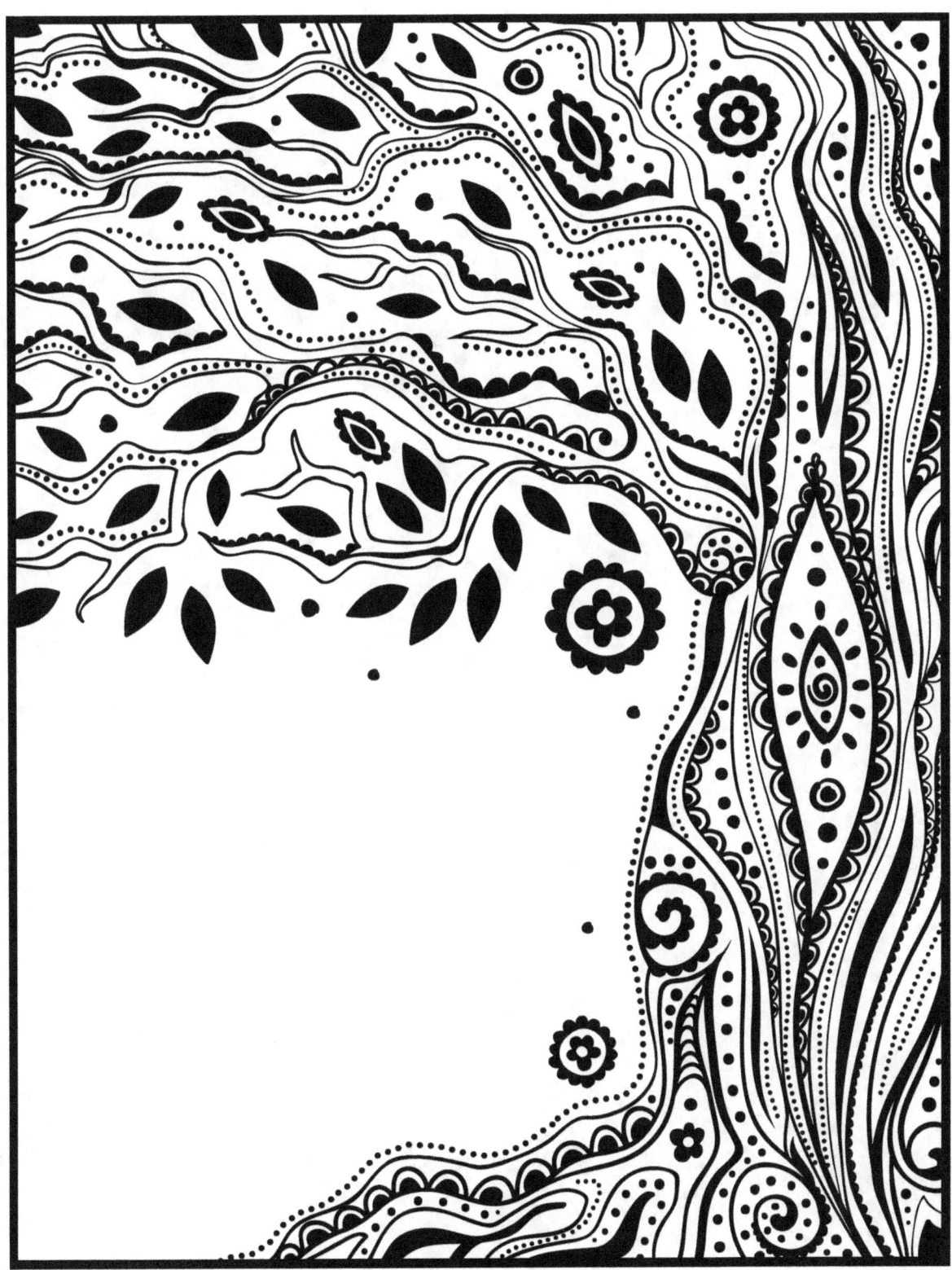

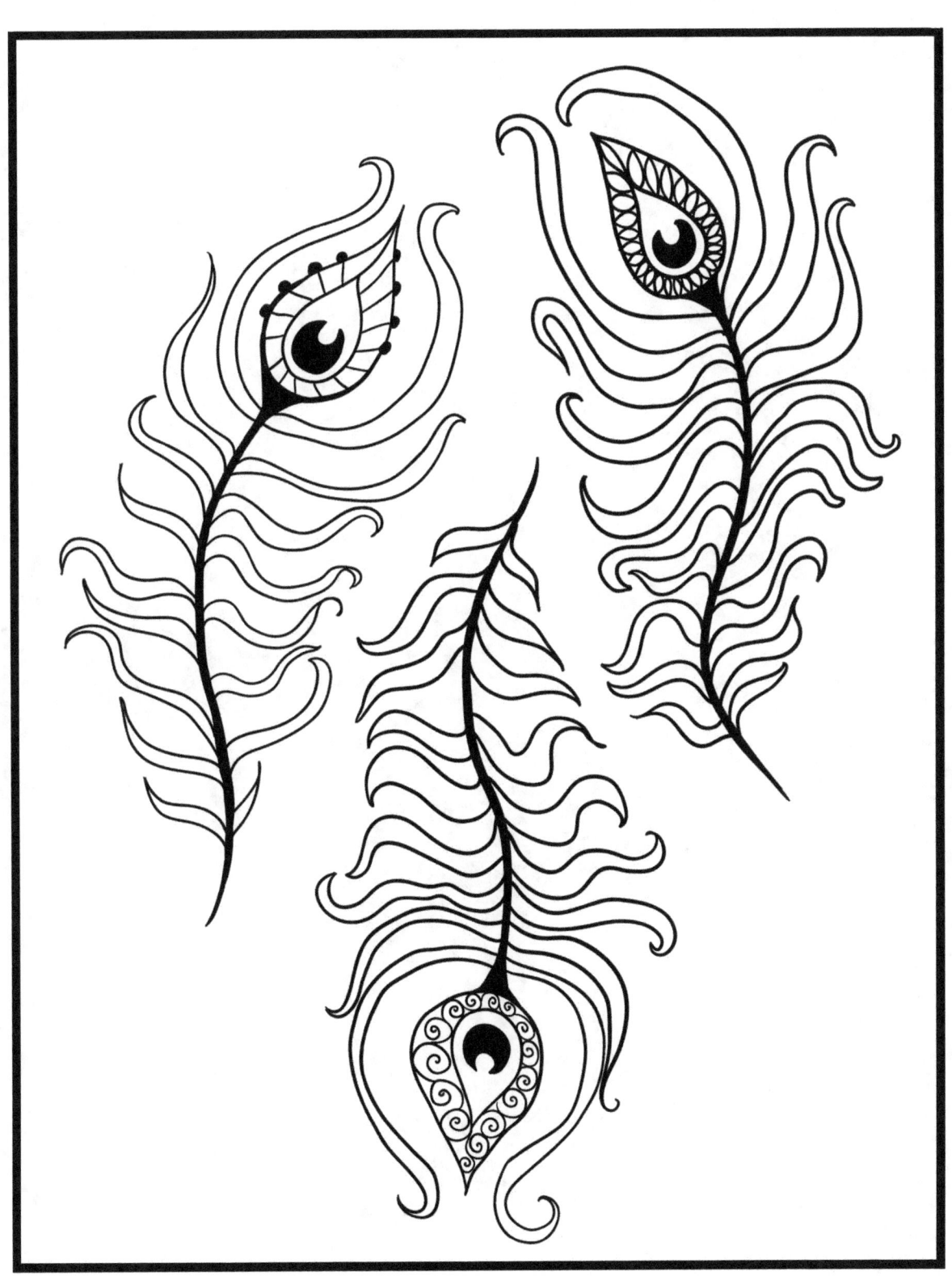

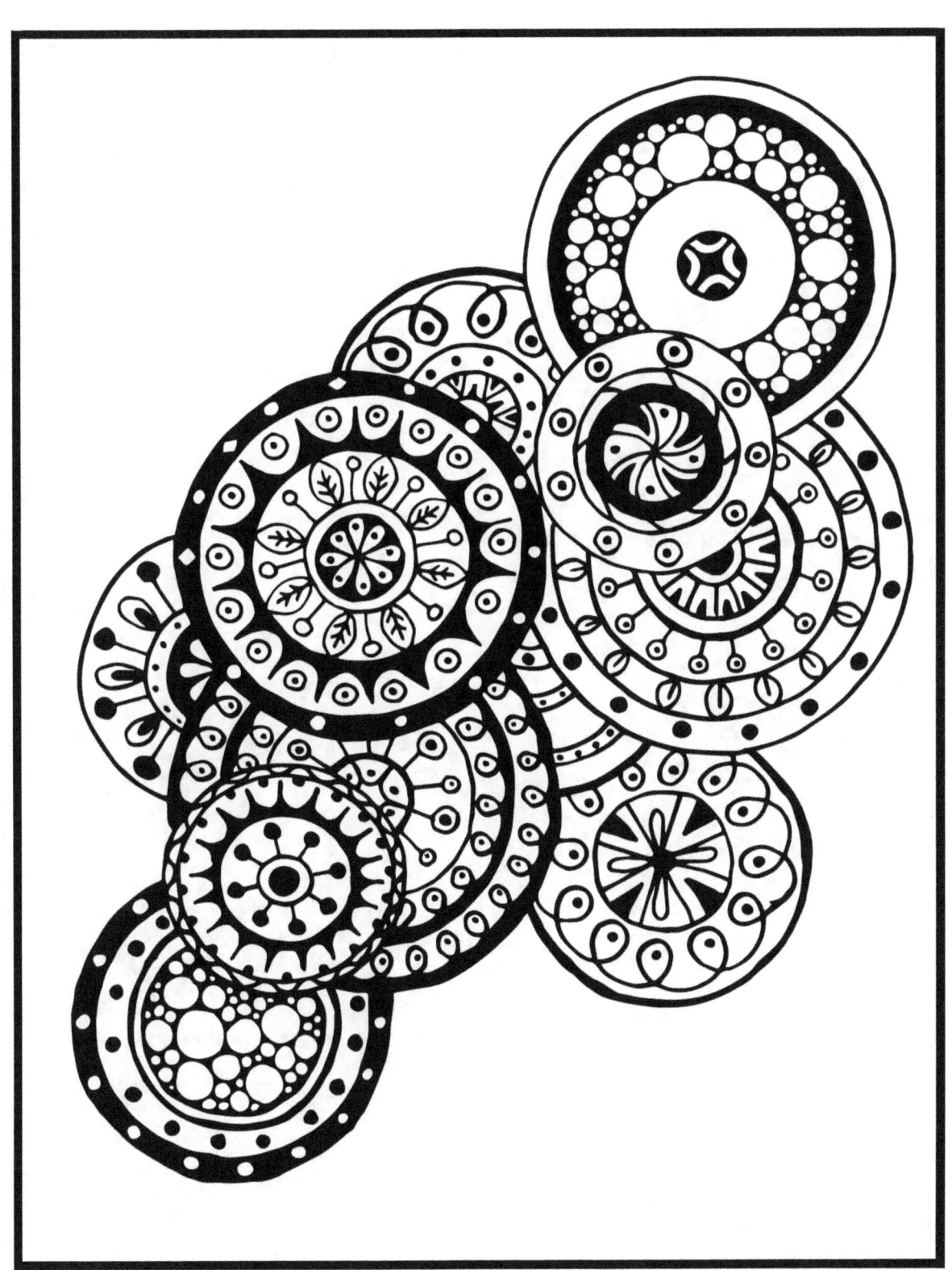

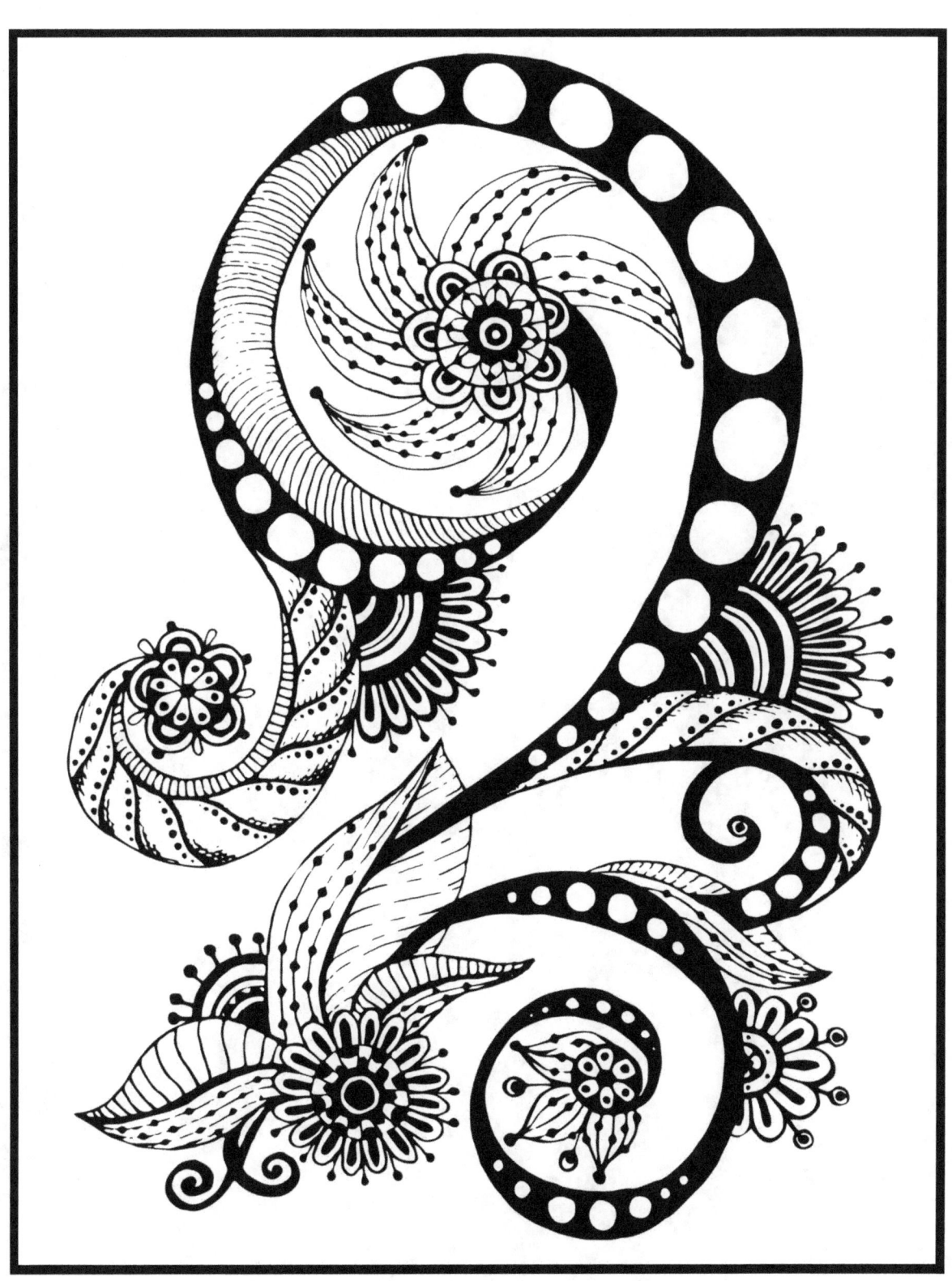

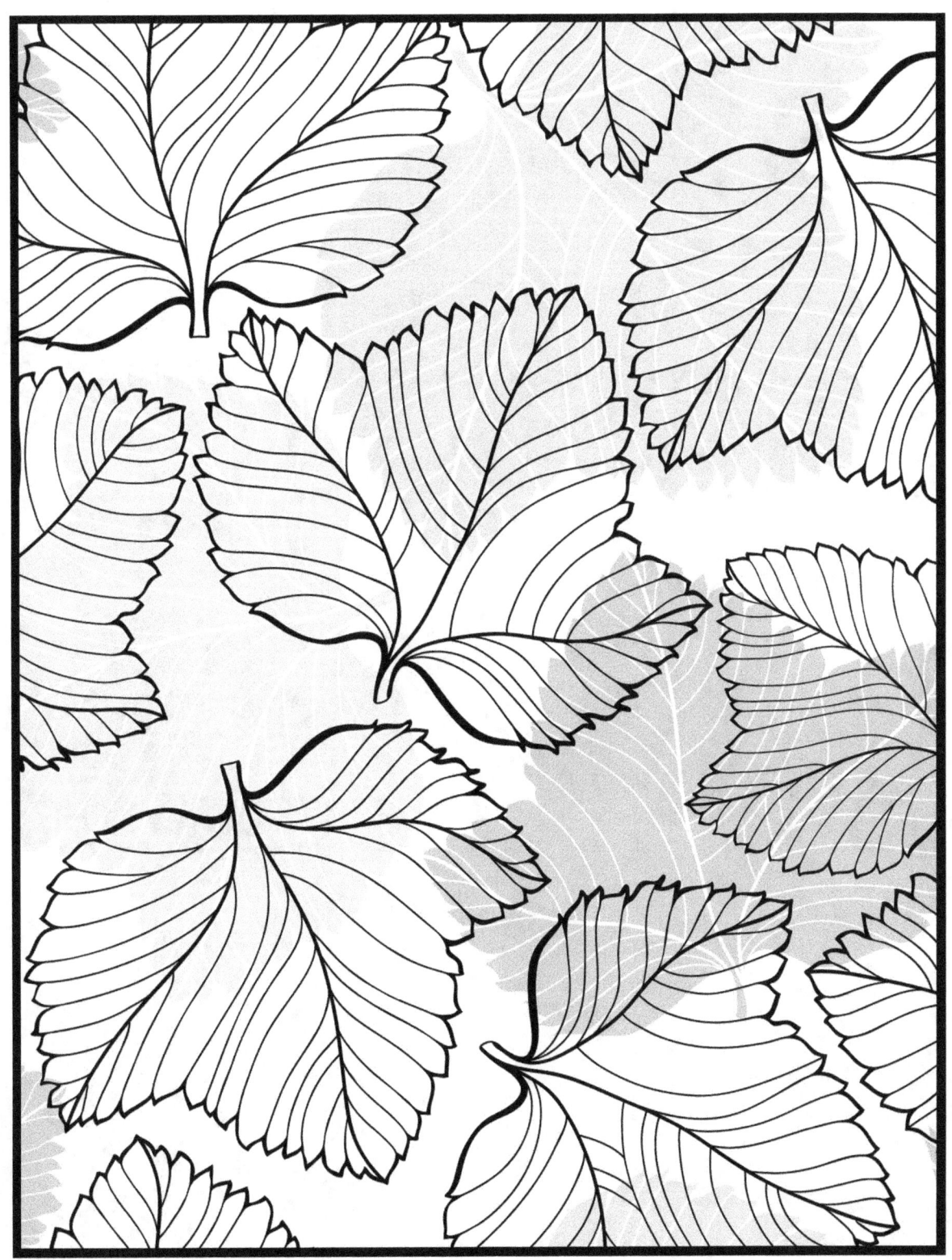

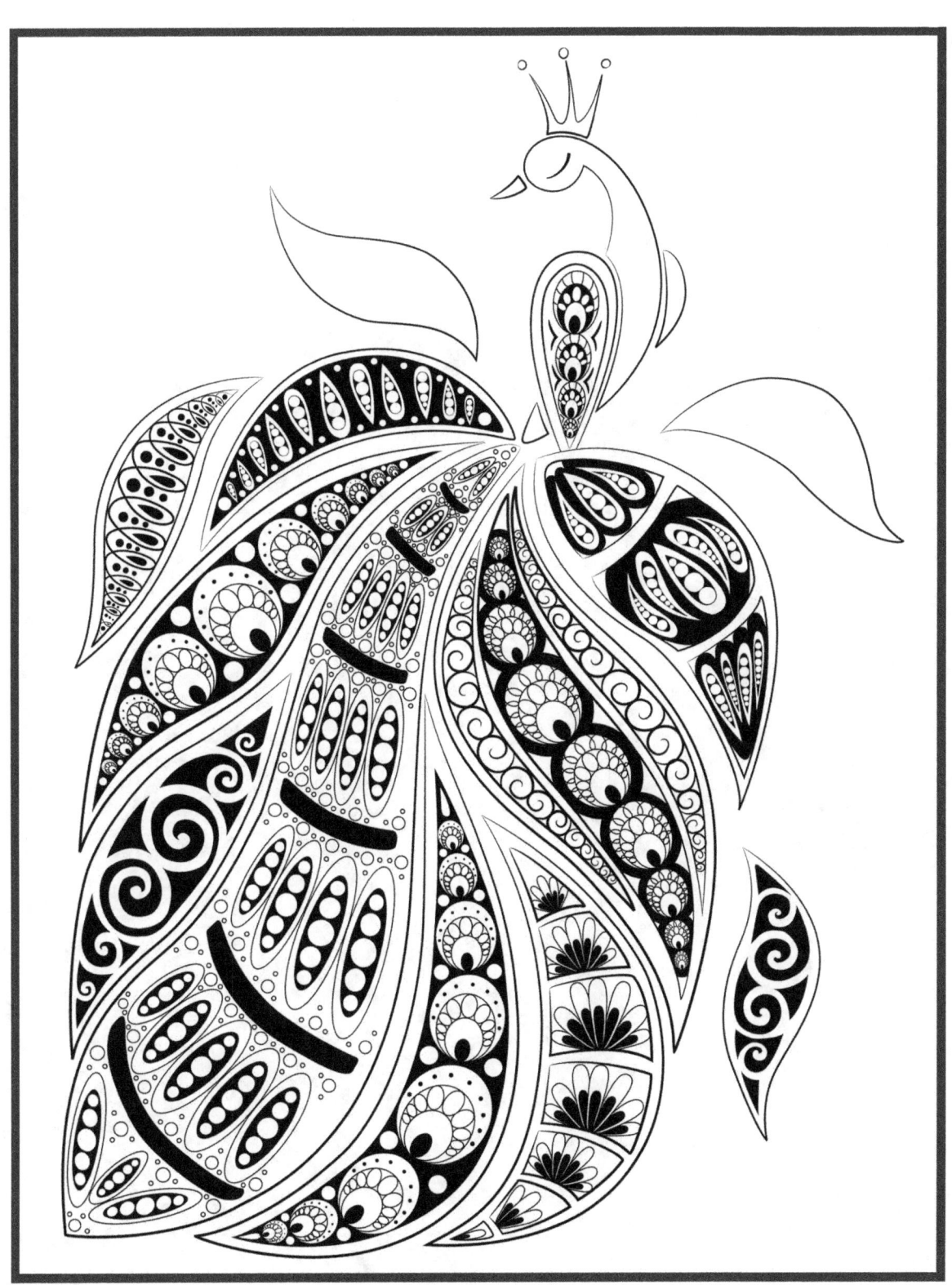

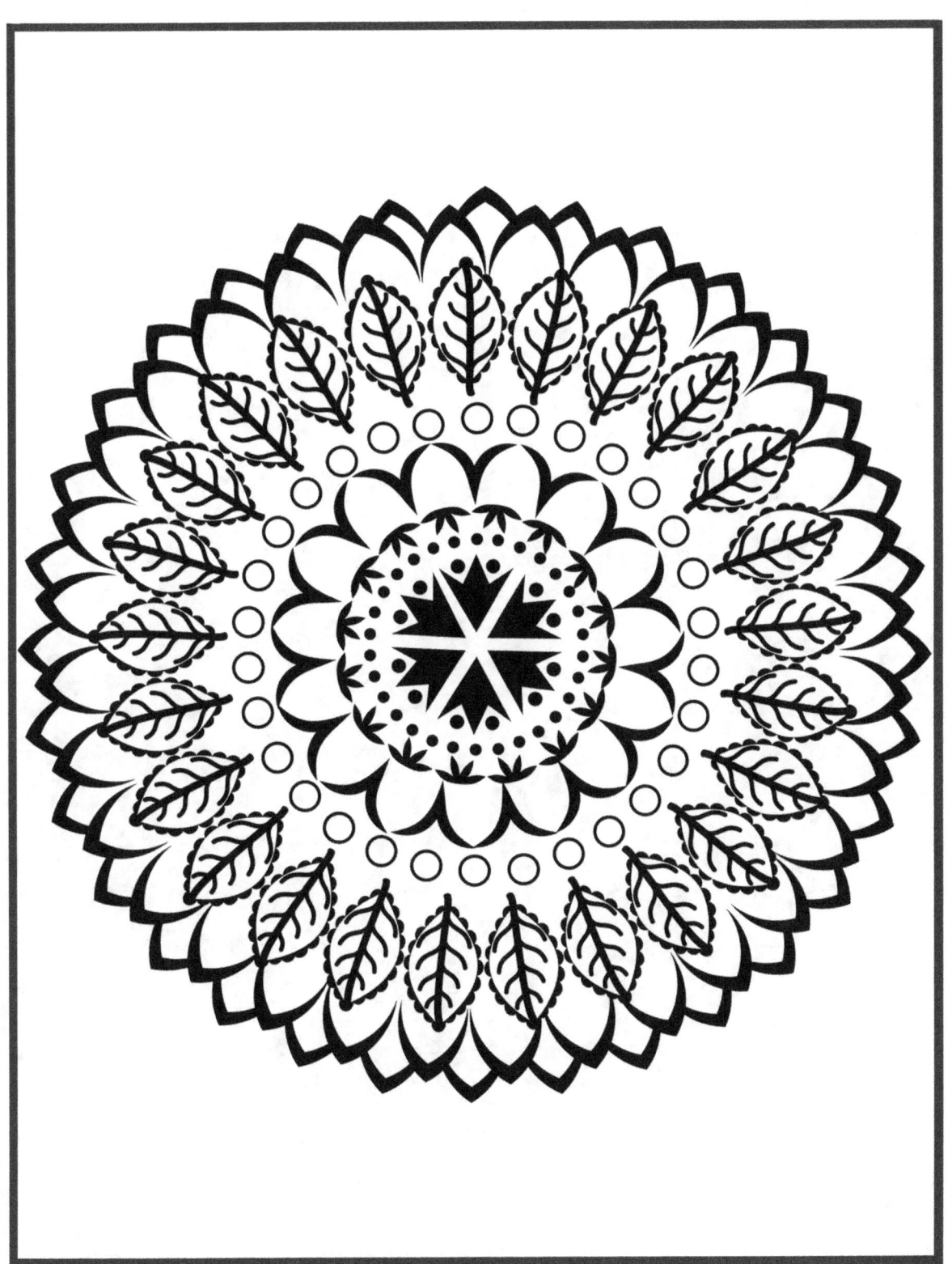

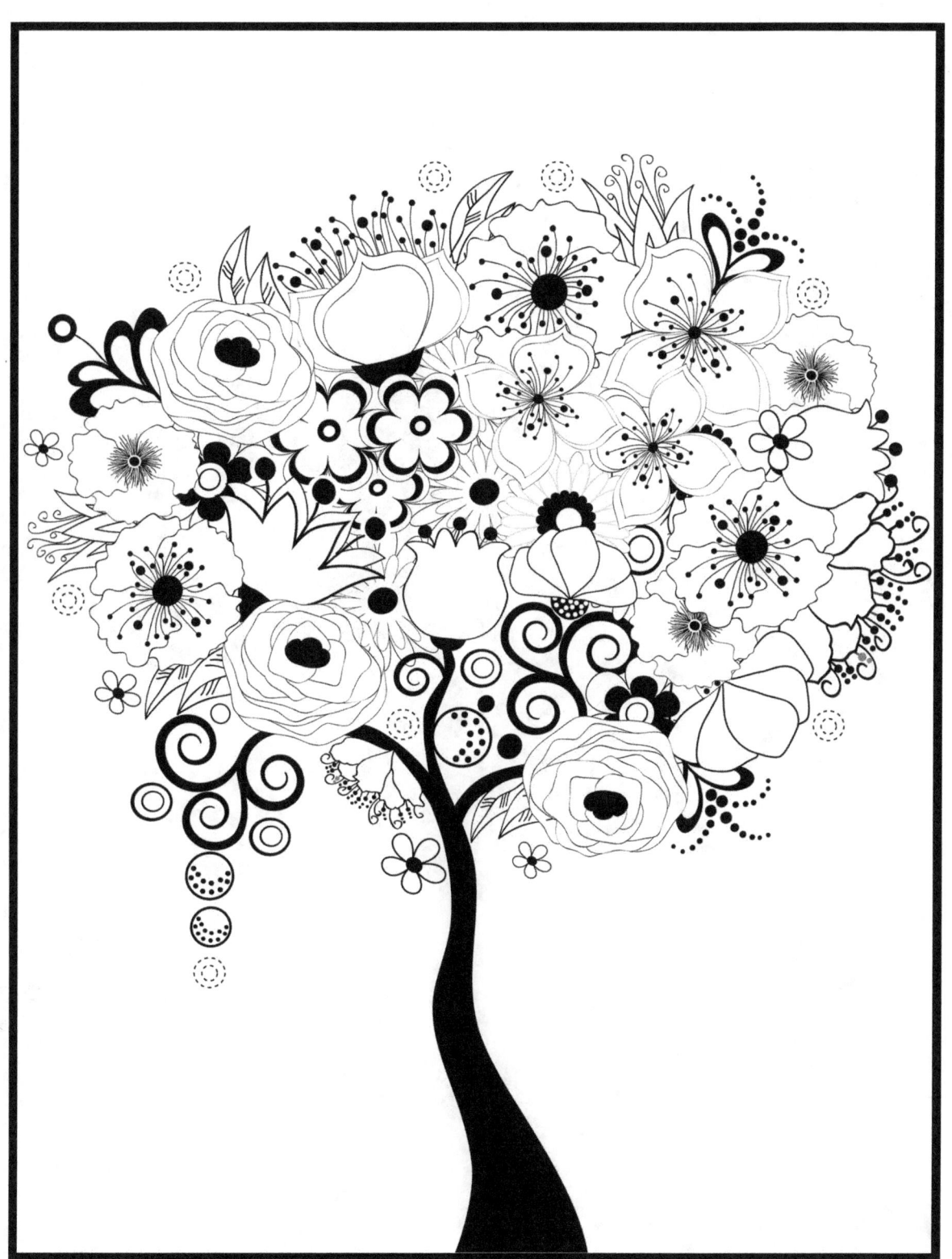

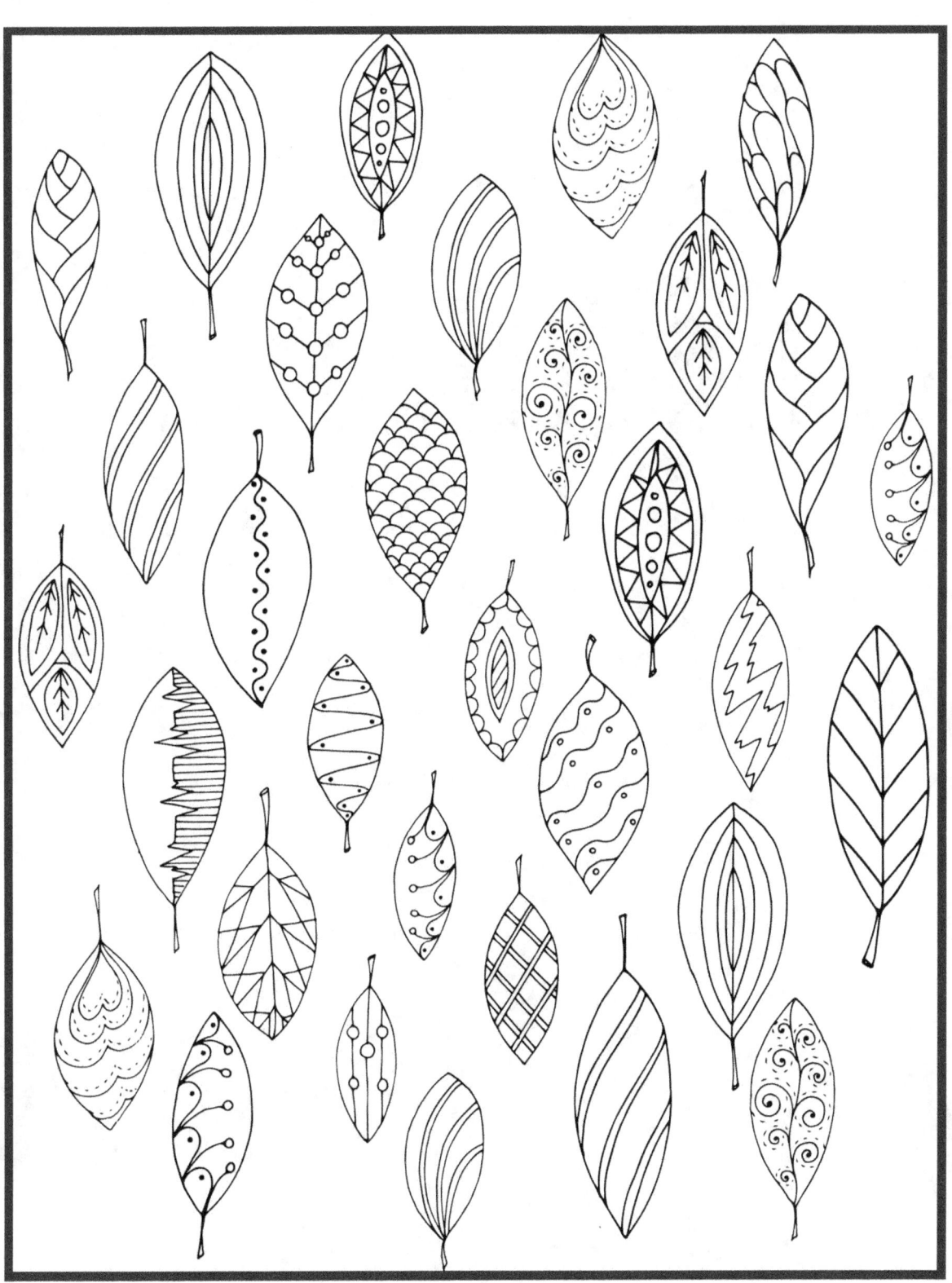

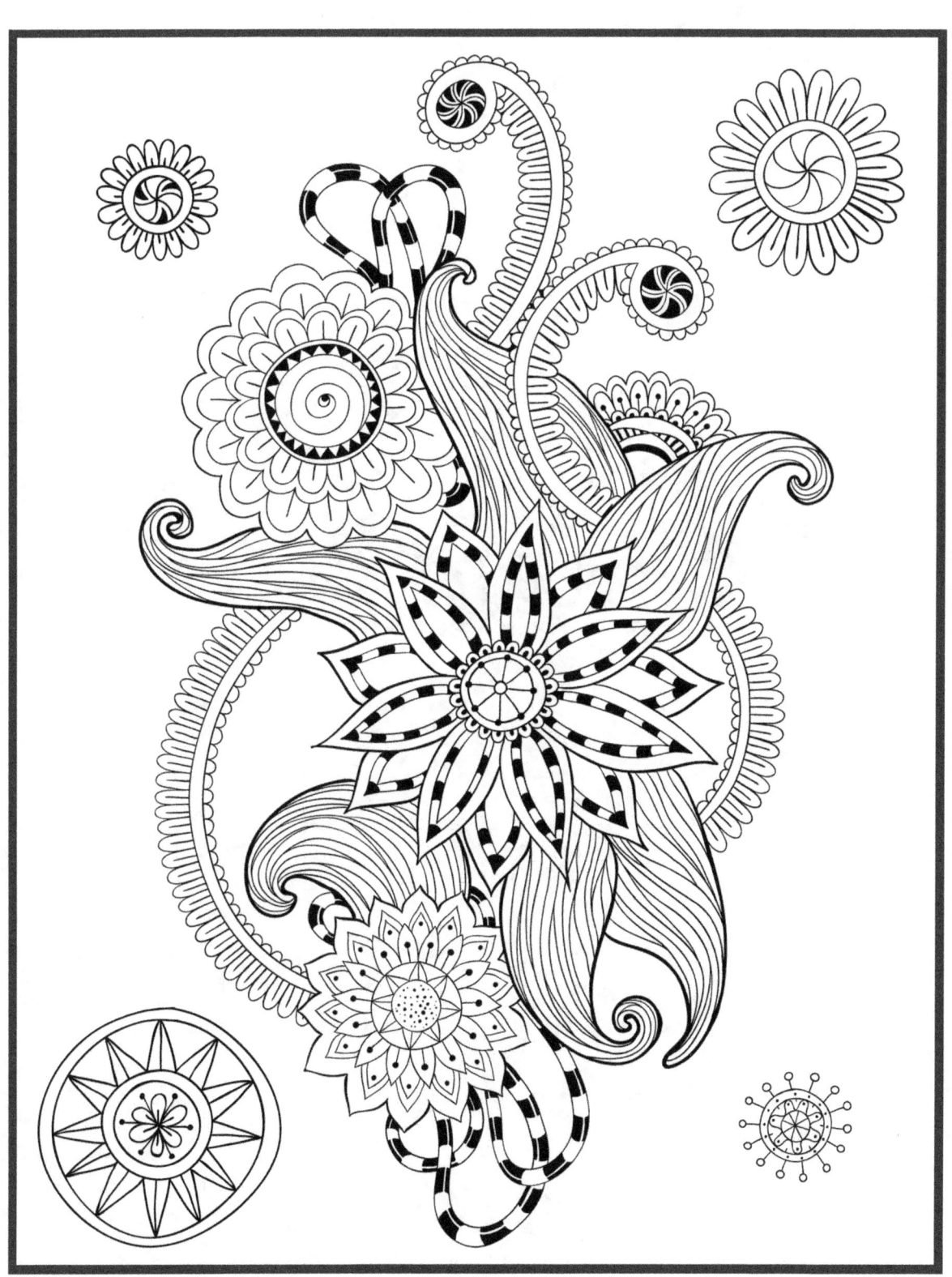

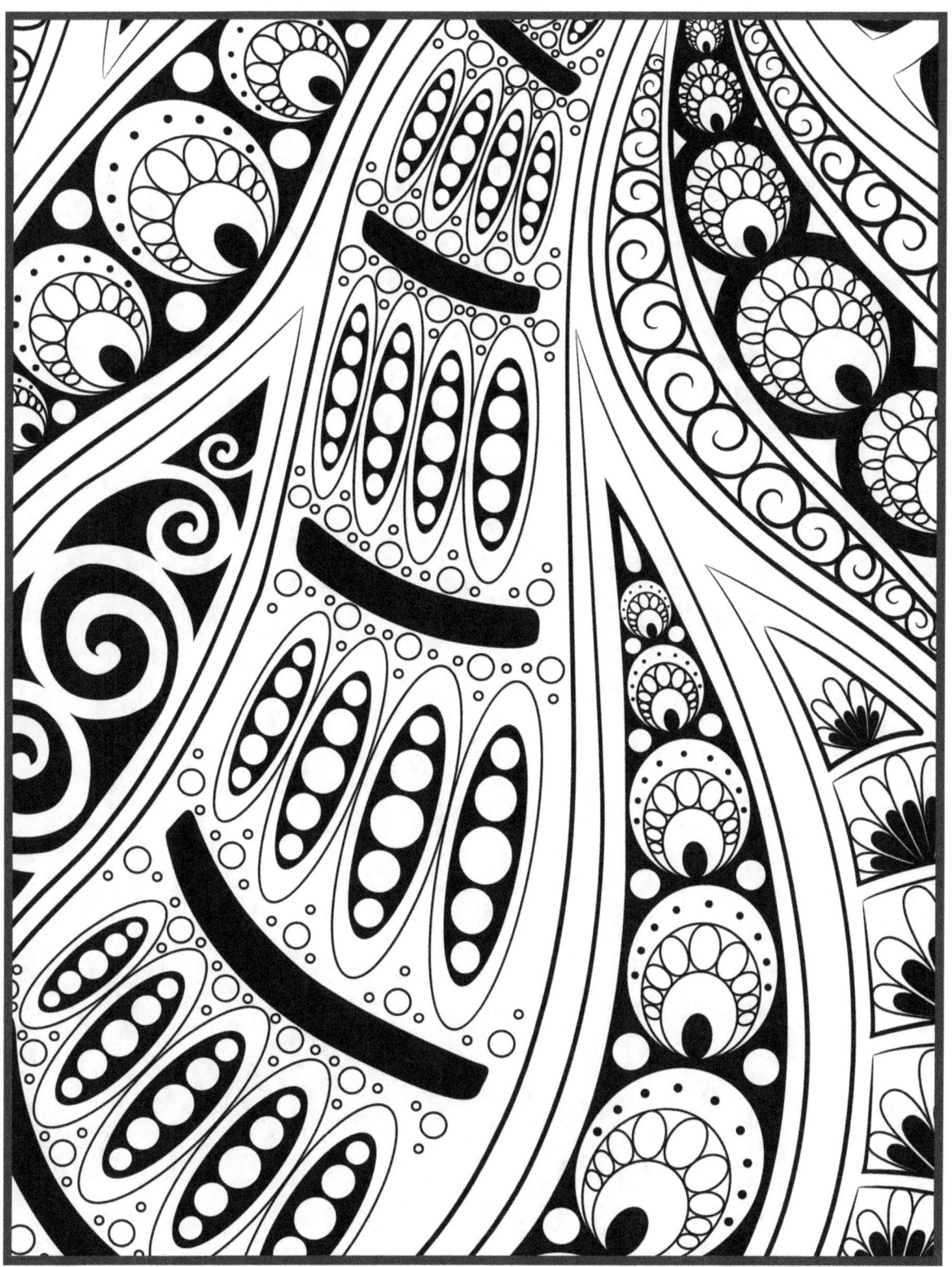

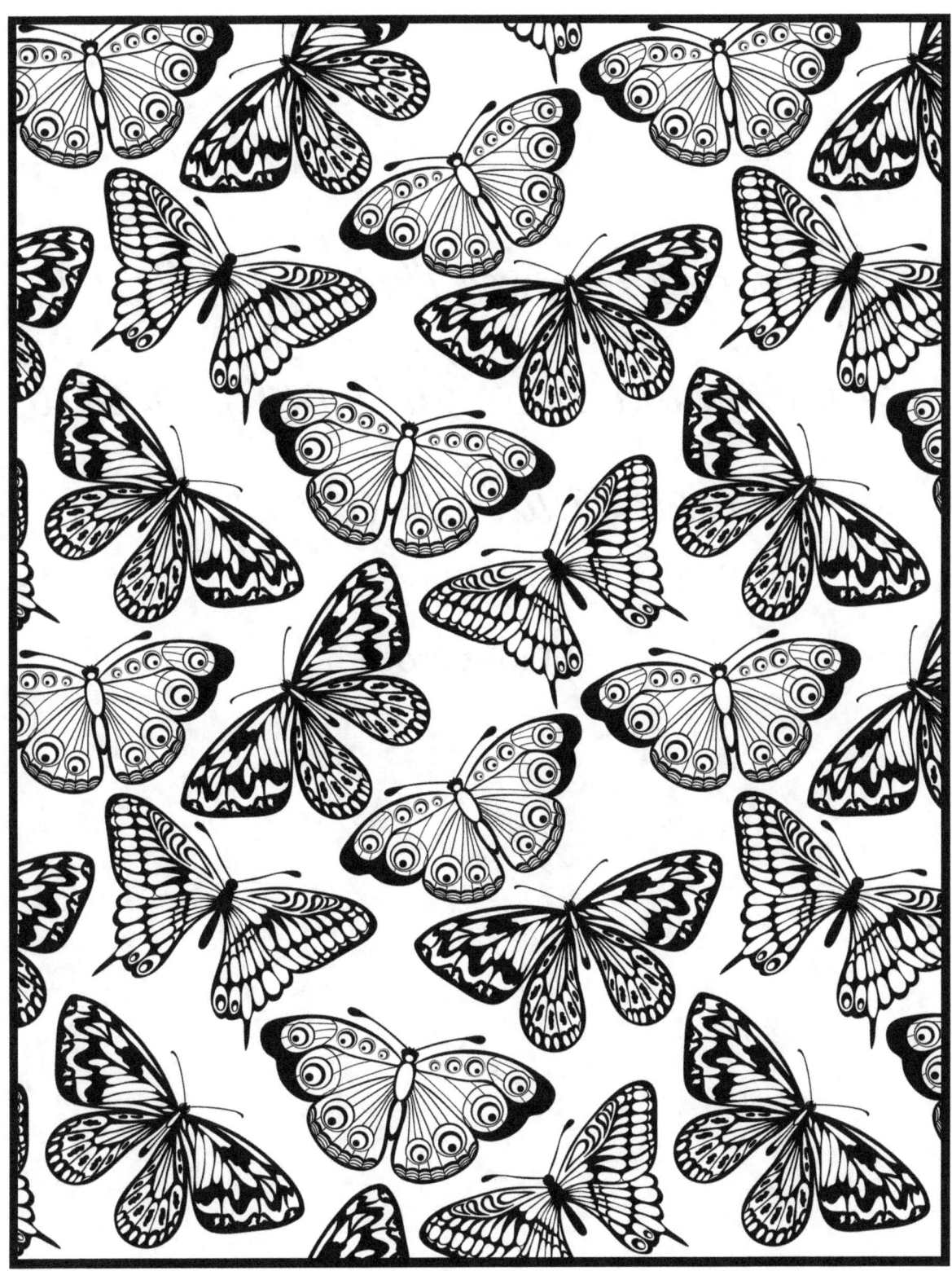

No one can see their reflection in running water. It is only in still water that we can see.

~ Taoist Proverb

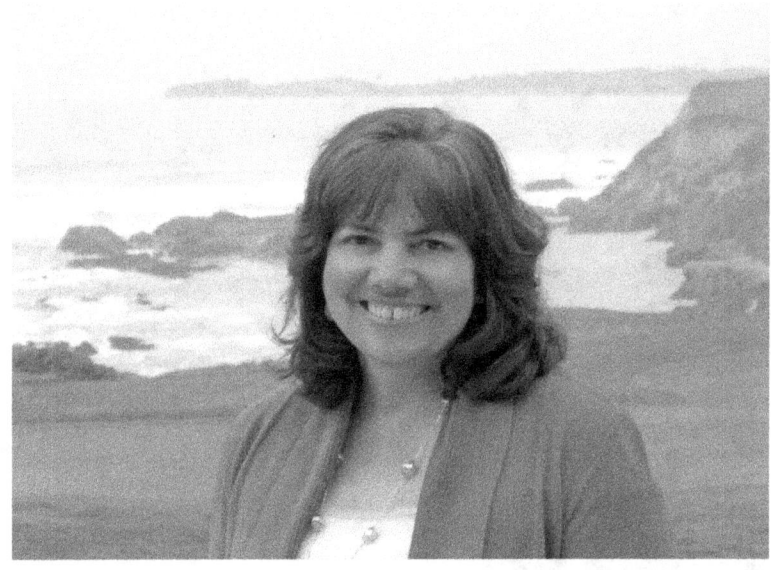

Barbara Freethy is a #1 New York Times Bestselling Author of 42 novels ranging from contemporary romance to romantic suspense and women's fiction. Traditionally published for many years, Barbara opened her own publishing company in 2011 and has since sold over 5 million copies of her books. Twenty of her titles have appeared on the New York Times and USA Today Bestseller Lists.

For more information, visit Barbara's website at www.barbarafreethy.com
Join her on Facebooks at www.facebook.com/barbarafreethybooks
Follow her on Twitter at www.twitter.com/barbarafreethy

www.ingramcontent.com/pod-product-compliance
Lightning Source LLC
Chambersburg PA
CBHW080821170526
45158CB00009B/2490